MW01006736

Scrupulosity

SCRUPULOSITY

Heal Your Mind,
Unbind Your Soul,
and Let God Work

Kevin Vost, PsyD

Our Sunday Visitor
Huntington, Indiana

Nihil Obstat
Msgr. Michael Heintz, Ph.D.
Censor Librorum

Imprimatur
✠ Kevin C. Rhoades
Bishop of Fort Wayne-South Bend
April 11, 2023

The *Nihil Obstat* and *Imprimatur* are official declarations that a book is free from doctrinal or moral error. It is not implied that those who have granted the *Nihil Obstat* and *Imprimatur* agree with the contents, opinions, or statements expressed.

Excerpts from the *Revised Standard Version of the Bible*—Second Catholic Edition (Ignatius Edition) Copyright © 2006 National Council of the Churches of Christ in the United States of America. Used by permission. All rights reserved worldwide.

Excerpts from the English translation of the *Catechism of the Catholic Church* for use in the United States of America Copyright © 1994, United States Catholic Conference, Inc.—Libreria Editrice Vaticana. Used with Permission. English translation of the *Catechism of the Catholic Church: Modifications from the Editio Typica* copyright © 1997, United States Conference of Catholic Bishops—Libreria Editrice Vaticana.

Every reasonable effort has been made to determine copyright holders of excerpted materials and to secure permissions as needed. If any copyrighted materials have been inadvertently used in this work without proper credit being given in one form or another, please notify Our Sunday Visitor in writing so that future printings of this work may be corrected accordingly.

Copyright © 2023 by Kathy Vost
28 27 26 25 24 23 1 2 3 4 5 6 7 8 9

All rights reserved. With the exception of short excerpts for critical reviews, no part of this work may be reproduced or transmitted in any form or by any means whatsoever without permission from the publisher. For more information, visit: www.osv.com/permissions.

Our Sunday Visitor Publishing Division, Our Sunday Visitor, Inc., 200 Noll Plaza, Huntington, IN 46750; www.osv.com; 1-800-348-2440

ISBN: 978-1-63966-004-9 (Inventory No. T2746)
1. RELIGION—Christian Living—Spiritual Growth.
2. RELIGION—Christian Living—Personal Growth.
3. RELIGION—Christianity—Catholic.

eISBN: 978-1-63966-005-6
LCCN: 2023933605

Cover design: Tyler Ottinger
Cover art: AdobeStock
Interior design: Amanda Falk

PRINTED IN THE UNITED STATES OF AMERICA

To all who feel heavily burdened, that in learning from Christ and bearing his sweet yoke, they will find rest for their souls.

Faith and reason are like two wings on which the human spirit rises to the contemplation of truth; and God has placed in the human heart a desire to know the truth — in a word, to know himself — so that, by knowing and loving God, men and women may also come to the fullness of truth about themselves.

— Pope St. John Paul II, *Fides et Ratio* ("Faith and Reason")

Acknowledgments

My thanks go first and foremost to editor extraordinaire Rebecca Martin, who not only proposed this book idea, but who proceeded to render my legions of linguistic infelicities a good deal more felicitous. Special thanks are also due to Rhonda Ortiz and Michael Baker for reviewing the text and providing plenty of helpful feedback. My gratitude extends as well to all the good people at OSV for bringing this text to print. As usual, I thank my author-friend Shane Kapler, always willing to provide insights and feedback on everything Catholic that I strive to bring to print. Special thanks as well to Father Wade Menezes, C.P.M., who graciously allowed me to reproduce his web article "Ten Commandments for Those Who Struggle with Scrupulosity," and who provided helpful comments to me on the section on the Sacrament of Reconciliation in this book's chapter 5. I also extend my gratitude to author-friend John Francis Clark for his willingness to review this book and provide his valued feedback. Finally, as always, this book would not exist in the papery (or electronic) flesh had not Kathy Ann Vost kept our house in order as I read, pondered, and prayed to better understand scrupulosity in hopes of healing minds, unbinding souls, and letting God work in our lives.

Contents

Introduction

What is Scrupulosity?
(and What Can We Do About It?)

These authors identified two dimensions of scrupulosity: (a) the fear of having committed a religious sin and (b) the fear of punishment from God. In most cases, the "sins" feared by individuals with scrupulosity present relatively minor religious or moral dilemmas and are not of central importance to overall religious observance.

— Jonathan S. Abramowitz, Ph.D.[1]

Do you fear sin and strive to avoid it? Do you dread God's punishment for sin? Do you fear offending God and letting him down? If so, so far so good! Every Catholic is called to strive to reject sin, to grow in virtue, and above all else, to love God with all that we are. When we do so in healthy and holy ways, accepting and employing God's graces, we will still

11

be beset with difficulties, with crosses we must bear. But our burdens will be lighter, and our yokes will be easier; our lives will be more peaceful and more fulfilling, and we will be better able to treat others with the kind of love that comes from proper love for ourselves.

On the other hand (or foot as the case may be), can you recall a time in which you have gotten a little pebble stuck in inside your shoe? Isn't it amazing how such a little thing can be so bothersome? If you are like me, the first chance you get, you pop off that shoe and shake the darn thing out. If you are in a situation where you can't remove it right away, the pebble occupies your attention so that it can be hard to focus on anything else.

Returning from pebbles to sins, the word *scrupulosity* itself derives from the Latin word *scrupulis,* which means "a small, sharp stone or pebble." People with scrupulosity walk around as if they have annoying little pebbles grating and irritating their very minds and souls, and they just can't seem to shake them out. Well, I'm no geologist, but a quick internet search shows there are three fundamental types of rock on the earth: igneous, sedimentary, and metamorphic. Within these three types we find more than seven hundred kinds of igneous rocks, and scads of different sedimentary and metamorphic rocks as well.

The psycho-spiritual "pebbles" that make up scrupulosity also come in a great number of varieties, though they too can be classed into a few common categories, such as: scruples of potential sins involving sexual, violent, or blasphemous thoughts; prayer practices; and reception of the sacraments, especially those of confession and the Eucharist.

As to the fundamental *psychological* nature of scrupulosity, our opening quotation — from a psychologist specializing in obsessive-compulsive disorders, including scrupulosity —

highlights that scrupulosity involves fear of sin and of God's punishment, but the quotation marks around "sins" in the second sentence make all the difference. While all good Catholics fear sin and the punishment it can bring, the "sins" the scrupulous fear are often not truly sins, but may involve very minor possible or potential infractions of the most inconsequential of religious or moral laws. They involve "sweating the small stuff," worrying over issues so small that they may not even be sins at all.

As to the fundamental *spiritual* nature of scrupulosity, St. Alphonsus Liguori says, "The suffering that affects scrupulous souls comes from the fear that what they are doing might be sinful." In other words, the scrupulous worry that their possible sins could jeopardize their eternal souls or even the souls of others.

Though we'll dig into this more throughout this book, I will note from the start that scrupulous thoughts and behaviors exist on a continuum. There are probably few among us who have not had what were or could have become scrupulous thoughts now and again, or at certain times during our lives. On the other hand, a small number of us may be so frequently and seriously troubled by scrupulosity that it meets the criteria for a subtype of a recognized psychiatric disorder, namely, obsessive-compulsive disorder (OCD). Many others may fall somewhere in the middle, with worries about possible sinful behaviors that may prove distressing at times though usually not debilitating.

In these pages I hope to provide helpful information that might be of assistance to those with seriously debilitating scrupulosity, to those who wonder if they may or may not be suffering from it, to those who have loved ones suffering with scrupulosity, and perhaps to therapists, pastors, or spiritual directors who strive to help ease the suffering of scrupulous souls.[2]

Flying from Scrupulosity on Wings of Faith and Reason

Our approach to conquering scrupulosity, at best, or enhancing our ability to endure it, at least, is guided by Pope St. John Paul II's eloquent words:

> Faith and reason are like two wings on which the human spirit rises to the contemplation of truth; and God has placed in the human heart a desire to know the truth — in a word, to know himself — so that, by knowing and loving God, men and women may also come to the fullness of truth about themselves.[3]

God crafted us beings who fly to truth — truth about him and about ourselves — through the powerful twin wings of faith and reason. God crafted us in his image and likeness as beings with intellect and will. He gave us reasoning minds that can unveil many truths, and he revealed many things directly to us that exceed the height attainable with unaided reason. Believing in him and what he revealed provides that wing of faith which, along with reason, can lift us all the way to heaven. In the words of St. Thomas Aquinas: "For when a man's will is ready to believe, he loves the truth that he believes, he thinks out and takes to heart whatever reasons he can find in support thereof; and in this way human reason does not exclude the merit of faith, but is a sign of greater merit."[4]

As we approach the truth about the psychological and spiritual phenomenon of scrupulosity, and how to overcome it, we'll do our best to unfold both wings: the wing of reason provided by the best scientific evidence in psychiatry and psychology, and the wing of faith provided by the teachings of Scripture, the Catholic Church, and our great Communion of Saints. Indeed, even some of the canonized saints who battled scrupulosity during their lives on earth have left behind their insights to help us fly to truth and peace. Further, they wait patiently up in heaven even now to help us battle scrupulosity, should we call upon them for their intercession.

Fearless Flying on the Wing of Faith

From the very first chapter, faith will be front and center as we'll strive to fly like eagles, moving away from scrupulosity upon the angel's wing of faith. Sometimes scrupulous thoughts and behaviors arise from misunderstandings of the true teachings of the Church. In each of our chapters we'll look at true, sound doctrines of the Faith as taught by our great Church Doctors — St. Thomas Aquinas foremost among them — and the Magisterium of the Catholic Church. Such truths may set some of us free from scrupulosity and help others to grow more deeply in their faith, even if they cannot quite shake every pebble from their soles (er, souls.)

As previously noted, many scruples involve supposed "sins" that may not be sins at all. That's why we will start in chapter 1 by examining just **what sin really is**, and how it differs from mere temptation.

Since we are called not only to fight sin, but to build virtue, chapter 2 will address the kinds of **moral virtues** we can build that can conquer, or at least temper, scrupulous thoughts and behaviors by sounding the call for the four high-flying cardinal virtues of fortitude, temperance, justice, and prudence.

God has infused our souls with yet higher supernatural, **theological virtues** of faith, hope, and charity (or love) that can help us defeat scrupulosity. These we'll address in chapter 3 — and as for "the greatest of these" per Saint Paul, even the pagan Virgil knew that *"amor vincit omnia"* ("love conquers all"), even scrupulosity.

Chapter 4 will unwrap seven special **gifts from the Holy Spirit** that can help battle scrupulosity. Indeed, even the least of these gifts (a mature and loving fear of the Lord) has been recognized by Church Doctors as a remedy for scrupulosity.

Virtues and gifts, as magnificent as they are, do not exhaust God's generosity and willingness to heal our souls from all that ail them. In chapter 5, we will look at the **seven sacraments** Christ gave to the Church. We will see how sacraments can provide the subject matter for scrupulous thoughts and behaviors, but also can be quite powerful spiritual balms.

In chapter 6 we will see that, depending on how it is understood and performed, **prayer** plays similar roles, either as a fertilizer or a pesticide for the shoots of scrupulosity. And we'll even find St. Thomas Aquinas's answer to the question: "If I get distracted while I pray, does God stop listening?" (And its follow-up for the scrupulous: "Does that mean I need to start over again?") Oh, and one last thing on prayer: The appendix will feature a specially-crafted prayer to help us counter scrupulosity itself, with the aid of God's generous superabundant grace.

When we use the wings of reason and faith to fly all the way to the truth, we encounter **Jesus Christ himself,** who is "the way, and the truth, and the life" (Jn 14:6). In chapter 7 we will find answers to questions like these: "WWJD?" as they say: "What would Jesus do if he were to give counsel to the scrupulous?" Further, "WDJD?" we might say: "What *did* Jesus do when he addressed the scrupulous?" After all, Jesus came so that we might have abundant life (Jn 10:10), to make us free (Jn 8:31), and to leave us in peace, so that our hearts would not be troubled or afraid (Jn 14:27).

Finally, when we conclude, we will contemplate one last time what it means to cast off needless fears and to wait with genuine, joyful hope for the day when we will come to meet the Lord.

Riding on Reason's Wing

Since scrupulosity has both religious and psychological components, to better understand it so that we can better cope with it, and in some cases overcome it, we will need to examine it in the light of psychological and psychiatric science too. We will need to unfold the wing of reason made sturdy and flightworthy by the intellectual virtues long acknowledged within the Catholic Church.

Aristotle and Saint Thomas spoke of a class of "intellectual virtues" that perfect our unique human reasoning capacities. They are *understanding, science* (or knowledge, from the Latin *scire* — "to know"), and *wisdom.* They appear together in Scripture as well, for example: "By wisdom a house is built, / and by understanding it is established; / by knowledge the rooms are filled / with all precious and pleasant riches" (Prv 24:3-4). Further, God is happy to provide the intellectual virtues to those who ask: "For the LORD gives wisdom; / from his mouth come knowledge and understanding" (Prv 2:6). And we *will* be asking him for them!

So, what are these three virtues that we'll call to our aid in defeating scrupulosity?

To put their nature in three nutshells, Saint Thomas tells us the following:

- **Understanding** denotes our capacity to grasp underlying principles and natures of things through abstract, conceptual thinking.
- **Knowledge** denotes the capacity to grasp cause and effect relationships through observation and chains of reasoning.
- **Wisdom**, the highest of them all, distinguishes itself "by judging both the conclusions of science, and of the principles on which they are based" (*ST,* I-II, q.57, a.2).

We will attempt to employ all three throughout every page of this book, but at the end of every chapter we will feature an essay that applies them to what the sciences of psychology and psychiatry have taught us about scrupulosity. For a few examples, in our first chapter-end essays, the virtue of *understanding* takes center stage as we explore the psychological nature of scrupulosity:

- What is scrupulosity's nature?
- What are its varieties?
- How does it manifest in thoughts, emotions, and behaviors?
- How does it relate to psychiatric disorders like obsessive-compulsive disorder and obsessive-compulsive personality disorders?
- How can we know if we have it? Is there some kind of self-test we can take?

As we move along in the book, the virtue of *science* will also have its say as we examine the cause-and-effect relationships involved in the psychology of scrupulosity:

- What are the causes of scrupulosity?
- Does religious belief cause scrupulosity?
- Does scrupulosity run in families?
- Is scrupulosity caused by our genes or our brains?
- Does one outgrow scrupulosity over time?
- Do people of various cultures and religions around the world suffer from scrupulosity?
- What effects does it produce in the scrupulous and their loved ones?

In our final Science of Scrupulosity essay, we will turn to the virtue of *wisdom* which judges the principles grasped by understanding and the conclusions derived from science, and determine what practical methods we can use to conquer or lessen scrupulosity. Still riding, at this point, upon the wing of reason, we will highlight and explain the best of modern psychological therapies for treating scrupulosity, answering questions like:

- What has research shown to be the most successful psychological treatments?
- How do they work?
- Can we employ them on our own?
- Do medications help?
- How can we tell if we should seek professional help? If so, what should we do?

Saintly Lessons for Scrupulous Souls

Ah, but there is a little bit more in store. After each chapter's Science of Scrupulosity essay, we will conclude with a Saintly Lesson for Scrupulous Souls — counsel from souls we know have made it to heaven, some after their own personal battles on earth with the snares of scrupulosity.

So, without further ado, shall we mount the wings of faith and reason to see what our minds can do to better know the enemy named scrupulosity, so that we might defeat it?

1

Certain Sin, Possible Sin, and the Difference Between Temptation and Sin

Sin is an offense against God. … Sin sets itself against God's love for us and turns our hearts away from it. Like the first sin, it is disobedience, a revolt against God through the will to become "like gods," knowing and determining good and evil.

— *Catechism of the Catholic Church* 1850

Let's begin by examining statements from psychological experts. Dr. Joseph W. Ciarrochi (1944–2010) was an expert in both the psychological and spiritual dimensions of scrupulosity. Let's look at the key idea in the following four sentences: "The term 'scrupulosity' refers to seeing sin where there is none.

Some call it a 'phobia concerning sin.' The person judges personal behavior as immoral that one's faith community would see as blameless. The dictionary defines a scruple as an ethical objection that inhibits action."[1] In other words, scrupulosity is:

- Seeing sin where there is none; i.e., it exceeds the normal Christian aversion to actual sin. It is frequently seeing mortal sin where there is only venial sin, a very important distinction we'll examine in depth in the pages ahead.
- A phobia regarding sin; i.e., a distressing, irrational fear about sin.
- A judgment of personal behavior as immoral that would be considered blameless by others of the same faith; i.e., a harsh judgment of acts that may not be contrary to the Faith.
- An ethical judgment that inhibits actions; i.e., it may interfere with important responsibilities in life.

The title of Dr. Ciarrochi's important book on scrupulosity is *The Doubting Disease*. Indeed, he notes that scrupulosity is called by this name in France.[2] This highlights another related feature of the nature of scrupulosity. When we are scrupulous, we may see sin where there is none, regarding thoughts or actions as sinful that other believers, and even the Church herself, would not consider so. In many cases, we feel we *cannot be certain* whether or not a particular thought, behavior, or failure to act is actually sinful, so we err on the side of presuming it was sinful. We live in a state of doubt that enhances our anxiety and may lead to assurance-seeking behaviors to help curb our doubts.

Perhaps at our last confession we forgot to confess some real (or possible) sin. Just in case, we decide we'd better go to confession again. Or, maybe we know we confessed the sin, but aren't sure we were contrite enough or that we prayed the prayers of penance with proper attention. Just in case, we decide we'd better go confess it again.

This brings out a common cycle found in those of us who struggle with scrupulosity. We encounter some distressing thought about any manner of possible sin — a fleeting illicit sexual thought, or an unwanted irreverent, violent, blasphemous, or sacrilegious image flashes across our mind. Because we are fearful of perhaps having sinned, we compensate in some way to reduce our anxiety. For example, by saying a particular prayer or set of prayers a certain number of times, or seeking out reassurance or forgiveness from a priest or spiritual advisor.

Let's move on to our second expert, David A. Clark, PhD:

> Given the prominence of sexual and religious themes in repugnant obsessions, we might expect the religiosity-OCD relationship to be especially strong in this symptom subtype. Moreover, it is commonly recognized that religious obsessions, or what has been called scrupulosity, represents a special type of obsessional problem that falls under the umbrella of repugnant obsessions.[3]

At times, we may all have fleeting immoral or repugnant thoughts that seem to come out of nowhere. For example: During your school years, did you ever have a hard time resisting the temptation to laugh out loud in class at the prompting of some class jokester, partly because you realized how inappropriate that might be? Have you ever thought of how embarrassing it would be to suddenly yell something out loud at a solemn occasion like a funeral? Such passing thoughts, though inappropriate, are not abnormal. Most of us, quickly recognizing the absurdity of such thoughts, move along to thinking about more appropriate things. But those of us with scrupulous tendencies tend to ruminate about such thoughts, worrying that they reveal something especially sinful in our nature. We worry that these thoughts will not go away, and that we might be compelled to act upon them. In psychiatric terminology, when such repugnant thoughts keep recurring, and we keep ruminating about them and fearing them, they are called *obsessions.* The rituals we perform to reduce the anxiety such thoughts produce are called *compulsions.*

If they occur often enough, last long enough, and produce enough disturbance in our emotions and in our life functioning, they may meet the first two criteria for what the DSM-5-TR — the latest edition of the Diagnostic and Statistical Manual of the American Psychiatric Association (2022) used to diagnose psychiatric disorders — calls obsessive-compulsive disorder (OCD). Though not every person with scrupulous thoughts will warrant a diagnosis of OCD, it is certainly worth our while to look at these criteria as we attempt to understand scrupulosity, at least, for the moment, in the most serious cases. We will look at the extremes of full-blown obsessive-compulsive disorder and the criteria required to meet it in the Science of Scrupulosity essay at the end of this chapter.

Having taken a brief look at scrupulosity through psychological lenses, zooming in on obsessions, compulsions, and doubts, let's lay some theological lenses on top and peer deep into the role that real or imagined sin plays in scrupulosity. Dr. Ciarrocchi posed the question, "Are scruples psychological or religious?" His answer was "yes."[4] It is generally both, since religious content lies at the heart of the scrupulous person's obsessions, anxieties, and compulsions. He calls scrupulosity "the pathology of Faith," a corruption and distortion of true Faith. The discomfort it brings can even lead some of us with scrupulosity to wonder if we are losing our minds (and thankfully, the answer here is "no").

Those of us with scrupulosity often realize — or are at least willing to consider — that our scrupulous thoughts are irrational and inconsistent with the true teachings of the Faith. But we can rarely be cured strictly through reasoning and the proper teaching of the Faith. Intellectual insight alone is not sufficient to cure scrupulosity. Indeed, as we will see in our first essay at the end of this chapter, even people diagnosed with obsessive-compulsive disorder may have good insight into their disorder. Still, there are many cases in which misunderstandings of the tenets of one's faith, and of the nature of sin itself, at the heart of scrupulous thoughts, diminished once the sufferer had grown in true understanding of the Faith. For example, many Catholic and non-Catholic Christians over the centuries have suffered scruples, wondering if could have inadvertently committed the unforgivable "blasphemy against the Holy Spirit" that Jesus refers to in Matthew 12:31. John Bunyan, the famous seventeenth century Protestant author of works including *The Pilgrim's Progress,* reported in his autobiography, *Grace Abounding to the Chief of Sinners,* not only of his fears of having committed a variety of sins, including the sin against the Holy Spirit, but of feeling urges to commit this sin. A proper understanding of what the Catholic Church teaches about *that* sin and, in fact, about *all* sin could help ease the conscience and the anxiety of the scrupulous who truly love God, but lack a thorough understanding of the nature of sin, and God's willingness to forgive all who ask him.

Understanding Sin

The *Catechism of the Catholic Church* (CCC) begins its catechesis on sin by defining it as "an offense against reason, truth, and right conscience; it is a failure in genuine love for God and neighbor caused by a perverse attachment to certain goods. It wounds the nature of man and injures human solidarity. It has been defined as 'an utterance, a deed, or a desire contrary to the eternal law'" (1849).

There is much to unpack here. In regard to scrupulosity, we

might note from the beginning that sin is an offense against not merely one's conscience, but "right conscience." Paragraph 1783 tells us that such an upright and "well-formed conscience" is educated by the authoritative teachings of the Church. Dr. Ciarrochi notes that during medieval times, scrupulosity was discussed in manuals of moral theology under the sections on "conscience." These medieval moral theologians taught that we are to follow the dictates of our conscience as informed by the stirrings of natural law and Church teachings on divine law. They also taught that we should not take actions with a doubtful conscience — yet the essence of scrupulosity is doubt. So, if the scrupulous person could not resolve their doubt, and continued to *feel* that objectively moral acts were wrong or objectively immoral acts were right, they were labeled as having an *erroneous conscience* about such matters. Since we are not bound to follow the dictates of an erroneous conscience, the scrupulous were told that they were *free to act without resolving the doubt.* For example, if a person with scrupulosity felt they should not receive Communion because *maybe* they left out a serious sin in their last confession, they would be advised to receive Communion anyway. This is the advice the scrupulous among us would most likely receive today.

Moving on in the *Catechism's* description of sin as a genuine failure in love of God and neighbor through a perverse attachment to certain goods that wounds us and our neighbor, we can begin to see more clearly how oftentimes the scrupulous "sees sin where there is none," per Dr. Ciarrocchi. Many of the supposed "sins" that the scrupulous fear clearly present no genuine failure in love for God or neighbor. Consider, for example, the common fear of having paid inadequate attention while praying, thereby disrespecting God. Who among us has not become distracted while thinking about or doing things aimed at nothing but our own pleasures? Just ask any golfer or other athlete.

Note too that sin is defined as "an utterance, a deed, or a desire contrary to the eternal law." Oftentimes the scrupulous may mis-understand just what is meant by *desire*. Does desire include, for example, any fleeting sexual image or thought? Is this what Christ meant when he said that, "every one who looks at a woman lustful-ly has already committed adultery with her in his heart" (Mt 5:28)?

Let's dig a little deeper into the true nature of sin in its two major varieties.

Mortal Sins that Kill the Soul

The word *mortal* — as in "mortal sin" — comes from the Lat-in *mors,* meaning "death." Mortal sins cause spiritual death and cut us off from God's grace, leading to damnation if we remain unrepentant. Committing a mortal sin means deliberately (not much room for doubt there) and selfishly turning away from God in favor of worldly goods. We read in the *Catechism* that three things are required for a sin to be mortal: "Mortal sin is sin whose object is grave matter and which is also committed with full knowledge and deliberate consent" (1857).

When we zoom in on those three things, we find:

- **Grave matter** (concerning very serious issues)
- Done with **full knowledge** that they transgress God's laws (not done in ignorance or doubt)
- and **Deliberate consent** (willfully chosen acts)

These are not the kinds of sins that we could rationally ponder or doubt if we've committed them accidentally. All three must be present at once for any mortal sin. If there is any reasonable doubt whatsoever on any *one* of the three conditions, one can rest assured that *no mortal sin has been committed.*

As for grave matter, our *Catechism* (1858) provides the ex-amples from the Ten Commandments that Jesus enumerated to the young man who asked what he must do to attain eternal life:

"Do not kill, Do not commit adultery, Do not steal, Do not bear false witness, Do not defraud, Honor your father and mother" (Mk 10:19). Clearly, deliberate harmful acts like murder, theft, slandering, or defrauding others are such grave matters that God issued explicit prohibitions against them. So too are gross sins of negligence, like failure to honor the parents who gave us life and cared for us when we were small and dependent.

Inoculating Ourselves from the Seven Deadly Sins

The Church has also long taught of seven capital or deadly sins. "They are pride, avarice, envy, wrath, lust, gluttony, and sloth or acedia" (CCC 1866). They are called deadly sins because they *may* become mortal sins, bringing death to the soul in the unrepentant. Some of their names and the "deadly" adjective might give pause to some scrupulous souls. Can eating too much junk food (gluttony?) or slouching on the couch for hours in front of the TV set (sloth?) land us in hell forever? Indeed, in a secular television series on the deadly sins years ago, its episode on sloth ended with the words: "If Christian Tradition is to be believed, the simple act of laziness can send you to hell!"[5] I don't know about you, but if that truly is the case, I'm in big trouble!

The key issue for those with scrupulous tendencies or for those of us with tendencies toward sin — that is, every one of us — is to know what these deadly sins really are.

Sloth and Scrupulosity Don't Mix

Sins of *sloth*, to begin with, are infinitely more serious than simple laziness (though laziness about certain matters can certainly flow from it). The key to understanding sloth starts with the word the *Catechism* gives us as its synonym, namely *acedia* which comes from the Greek word meaning "without care." The deadly sin of sloth specifically means spiritual sloth; in essence, saying through our thoughts and actions: "God, I don't care!" It is a spiritual boredom and apathy for the things of God, rather than merely laziness or indolence that avoids physical exertion. Indeed, a super-lean exercise fanatic may be spiritually slothful if he or she zooms around the gym or the open roads for hours at a time, while failing to give God his due. True sloth can be serious business. In fact, Thomas Aquinas tells us it directly opposes the first great commandment to love God with all that we are. I would opine that almost by definition, those actively battling with scrupulosity are highly unlikely and virtually unable to suffer from spiritual sloth or *acedia*. They certainly do care about the things of God, but needlessly fret over thoughts, words, and deeds that may not be sins and may not bother God in the slightest.

More to Gluttony than Meets the Palate

Moving along to gluttony: It means more than simply eating too much junk food, or even healthy food for that matter. St. Thomas Aquinas tells us that it is an inordinate, unreasonable desire for food that can entail more than simply desiring to eat too much. There are different "species" or varieties of the vice of gluttony that include the tendency toward eating too much, but also the habit of eating too greedily by wolfing down our food, eating too hastily by eating too often, as well as eating too sumptuously or too daintily, demanding gourmet foods while showing ingratitude for plain and simple fare. Gluttony's potential toward deadly sin comes from the fact that it can divert our attention from God by focusing so much on what goes into our bellies. Also, many philosophers and theologians saw it as a "gateway sin" toward sins of lust by weakening our control over our bodily appetites.

Still, in a very perceptive observation, Saint Thomas notes:

> The vice[6] of gluttony does not regard the substance of food, but in the desire thereof not being regulated by reason. Wherefore if a man exceeds in quantity of food,

not from desire of food, but through deeming it necessary to him, this pertains, not to gluttony, but to some kind of inexperience. It is a case of gluttony only when a man knowingly exceeds the measure in eating, from a desire for the pleasures of the palate. (*ST*, II-II, q.148, a.1)

Just because one is overweight or believes he eats too much, this does not necessarily mean he is in the thralls of the potential deadly vice of gluttony. Indeed, as I've recently explained in detail elsewhere,[7] recent scientific research provides strong evidence that some of the kinds of foods we have been advised to eat by experts and governmental bodies over the last several decades — e.g., ultra-processed and high carbohydrate foods — can, through their actions on hormones like insulin, glucagon, and ghrelin, actually stimulate our appetites and decrease our natural urges to exercise, thus *simulating* "sins" of both gluttony and sloth. Therefore, impaired physiology, and not abnormal psychology or immoral choices, may often be to blame for our voraciousness and laziness!

Harking back to Saint Thomas's quotation, we have not necessarily eaten excess food due to gluttony, but because we have "deemed" the kinds of foods we've been advised to eat "as necessary" to us, due to "some kind of inexperience." The kind of inexperience that makes all the difference is the lack of experience of what it feels like and of what happens to our bodily temples when we primarily eat the foods God created for us to eat.

Demoting the Captain of Lust

As for sins of lust, they, along with gluttony, have been classed as "carnal" or "bodily" sins, since they arise from the natural stirrings of the flesh, while pride, avarice, envy, and wrath have been classed as "spiritual sins," since they directly involve the soul rather than the body (though our bodies can be used as instruments to act out these "spiritual sins"). The spiritual sins have also been considered more likely to lead to graver sins than those of the body, though the bodily sins are often hardest to resist because they are perversions of our natural drives — nourishment and reproduction — that are good for us as individuals and as members of the human species. Still, if you'll forgive a personal note, when I have given live talks on the seven deadly sins and asked audience members for a show of hands for what they consider the top three deadly sins causing the most havoc in our world today, sins of lust have won every time.

All of the seven deadly sins are also called "capital sins." This derives from the Latin word *caput*, meaning "head." When we speak of capital sins, we are using *head* in the sense of the person who forms the goals, issues the commands, and gets the ball rolling. This tradition harkens back to some elegant imagery from Pope St. Gregory the Great's *Moralia* commenting on the Book of Job: "When the trumpet sounds, he says, 'Aha!' / He smells the battle from afar, / the thunder of the captains, and the shouting" (Jb 39:25). Gregory portrayed the seven deadly sins as captains, and at times as generals, leading a vast and deadly army. The soldiers are a multitudinous variety of sins and misdeeds, and the capital sins are the officers who set them to their nefarious tasks. Gregory builds all this dramatic moral exegesis on that verse of a mighty horse that smells a battle coming and hears the thunder and shouting of approaching evil captains with their deadly hordes.

Lust, though a carnal rather than a spiritual sin, can indeed be a deadly captain if it issues commands to soldiers who commit acts like adultery or murder. We saw this long ago in the story of King David and Bathsheba, though we must recall that after his repentance, God in his loving mercy was willing to forgive the adulterous, murderous king. In our time, sadly, some sins of lust may lead to the killing of unborn babies. Even in such cases, God will forgive the repentant.

The woes of lust weigh heavily upon the minds of many scrupulous souls. Many worry over the natural, fleeting sexual temptations which virtually everyone deals with now and then. A smaller subset of scrupulous souls are beset by recurrent, repugnant thoughts that they might perform grossly abhorrent sexual actions, like sexual improprieties with children or persons of the same sex. We will examine both kinds of sexual scruples in more depth in our next section differentiating between temptation and sin.

Scrupulosity and the Other Deadly Spiritual Sins

Any of the other of the seven deadly sins, along with sloth, gluttony, and lust, may provide fodder for scrupulous thoughts in a variety of ways:

- **Avarice** (or greed): The *Catechism* lists this sin as avarice, deriving from the Latin *avere,* meaning to desire or crave (see 1866). The Greek Fathers called it *philarguria,* literally meaning the love of silver — *argyos.* St. Thomas Aquinas describes it as "an immoderate love of possessing." Some scrupulous souls may fear they are too greedy or that they have been too stingy in giving to the Church or other charities.

- **Wrath**: In Saint Thomas's Latin, he used the word *ira* for excessive, inordinate anger. We still see it in English when we speak of something raising someone's "ire" or making them "irritable." Some scrupulous souls may fret and obsess over inappropriate outbursts in their own past, fearing that the subject of their wrath, and God himself, may never forgive them. They may fear that any feelings of anger are sinful, but here they should know well that Saint Thomas distinguishes between the normal and appropriate human passion of anger and the inappropriate, excessive vice or sin of wrath. Echoing Aristotle, Thomas notes that there are times when we should feel anger, as in cases of injustices toward our neighbors or toward God. When we feel anger, it should be directed at the right person (the offending party), at the right time (after we have paused to allow the height of our anger to pass), and for the right reasons (to correct the offender and protect the innocent, rather than to harm the person who angered us).

- **Envy**: Pope St. Gregory the Great entered envy into the list of the deadly sins, using the Latin word *invidia,* meaning to look upon. Whereas *jealousy* regards our sadness at the prospect of losing some good of our own, *envy* entails a sorrow in response to another person's good. In this way it opposes the second great commandment to love our neighbors as ourselves. As brothers and sisters in Christ, indeed as "one body in Christ" (Rom 12:5), we are to "rejoice with those who rejoice," and "weep with those who weep" (Rom 12:15). For those free from scrupulosity, Saint Paul's words should remind us to show compassion for our brothers and sisters who are suffering from it, to strive to lighten their load and give them reason to rejoice.
- **Pride**: The Latin word for pride is *superbia,* and Saint Thomas says, "it is so-called because a man thereby aims higher (*supra*) than he is" (*ST,* II-II, q.162, a.1). Saints Gregory and Thomas call pride the "queen of

the vices," because if we choose to spurn God and place our own desires above his, it can call forth all manner of sins in its service. Most scrupulous souls do not consciously see themselves as trying to place themselves above God — quite the contrary, in fact — since they are often so fearful of having contradicted or neglected his Divine Will in the smallest of ways in thought, word, or deed. Yet a certain form of pride will manifest in struggles and difficulties in accepting the guidance and reassurance of spiritual directors and wise teachers within the Church, believing they must fix themselves through their own psychological and spiritual resources, pulling themselves toward heaven by their own bootstraps through the various compulsive acts. Certainly, a true sense of humility, achieving a "golden mean" of virtue regarding both what we can do on our own, and what requires our submission to God and his human instruments on earth, is needed to combat the kind of pride that may accompany scrupulosity. Indeed, humility, being the "mother of virtues," can help us crush the "queen of the vices," and provide real succor to the scrupulous among us. In our next two chapters we will take a closer look at the two holy bookends of humility and charity.

Venial Sins that Burn Like Straw

We should all be aware that by no means are all sins, though real, mortal or deadly. Saint John tells us about "sin which is deadly" but also "sin which is not deadly" (1 Jn 5:16–17). Non-mortal, venial sins — from the Latin word *venia*, meaning "pardonable" — are smaller moral transgressions regarding less serious matters, or even serious matters done without full knowledge and consent. They involve an inappropriate or "disordered affection for created goods" (CCC 1863) that weakens charity, but does not separate us from God's friendship and sanctifying grace. They do not entail a deliberate turning away from God, but, per St. Thomas Aquinas, "by venial sins man's affections are clogged, so that they are slow in tending towards God" (*ST*, III, q.87, a.1). They involve less serious matters and may be committed on the spur of the moment without deliberation — for example, blurting out cuss words after stubbing your toe, or yelling at someone who bumped into you or accidentally damaged or broke something of yours. Virtually any sin that could fall into the category of the seven deadly sins might merely be venial, depending upon the particulars of the situation and one's behavior.

Venial sins merit temporal punishment while here on earth, or after death in purgatory, being the "wood, hay, and straw" that will be cleansed by fire and will not ultimately deprive us of life in heaven with God (see 1 Cor 3:12–15). Still, repeated venial sins can plant the seeds of vicious habits, in which mortal sins can take root.

Venial sins may certainly be the focus of scrupulous thoughts, though we should recall that such sins do *not* have to be confessed in the Sacrament of Reconciliation. Indeed, we might recall as well that through the *Confiteor* prayer, or the Penitential Rite, in which we confess our sins to God and our neighbors, along with Communion and other prayers of the Mass, God does forgive venial sins, though mortal sins require sacramental absolution in confession.

Though every Catholic — whether suffering from scrupulosity, completely free from it, or somewhere in the middle — should understand the general nature of the different kinds of sins and ways in which the Church can help us overcome them, we must recall that scruples often involve, as St. Alphonsus Liguori made clear, acts that the scrupulous fear "might be sinful," and acts that Dr. Ciarrochi has noted may truly not be sins at all. We'll turn next to one way to help us all make a crucial distinction: the difference between temptation and sin.

Temptation vs. Sin

There's a real world of difference and a series of steps between temptation and sin, and we should all keep in mind that, from the start, mere temptation is not sin (and neither are intrusive thoughts that pop up without our prompting). Early in the history of the Church, Desert Fathers — and yes, Desert Mothers too, as we'll see in a page or two — fled life in cities to live holy lives of semi-isolation in the sandy deserts of Egypt and the Middle East. Evagrius of Pontus (AD 345–399) was one such man who did so, gaining great insight into temptation and sin, and indeed, becoming the first theologian to provide insights into what would become known as our aforementioned seven deadly sins.

Ancient biographies relate that, early in his life, Evagrius was consumed with vanity due to the praise and acclaim he received for his powers as a preacher. He was also so beleaguered by recurrent thoughts of infatuation with a married woman that he eventually fled Constantinople to a monastery near Jerusalem. There he received spiritual guidance from Melania the Elder (AD 350–410), who had founded a religious community of women on the Mount of Olives. Evagrius joined a monastic community in Nitria in Lower Egypt, and finally, in his last years of life, he lived in another monastic community deep in the heart of the Egyptian desert.

I imagine we can all agree that life in cities is certainly full of temptations, and even 1,600 years ago, Evagrius discovered the same. He fled city life but found, as did his Savior before him, that even the depths of the desert provide no sure relief from evil temptations. Despite their daily life of prayer and work while living in small, isolated huts, and despite their desires for holiness, being fallen human beings, Evagrius and his religious brothers were still often assaulted by temptations toward various kinds of sins.

In his *Practical Treatises,* Evagrius wrote about eight evil *logismoi* (thoughts) that would assail him, most of which would come down to us in Pope St. Gregory the Great's list of the seven deadly sins.[8] In addition to his influence on the development of the list of the seven capital or deadly sins, he provided an important insight from the start in describing them as "assailing thoughts." Of course, the scrupulous are attacked or assailed, so to speak, by scrupulous thoughts — but such thoughts, in and of themselves, are not sins.

Another Eastern (Greek-writing) Church Father who contributed greatly to our understanding between the difference of temptation and sin was St. John Climacus (579–649). In his beautiful spiritual classic, *The Ladder of Divine Ascent,* he describes a metaphorical ladder of 33 steps (corresponding with the number of years Jesus lived on earth) through which we acquire a series of virtues and learn how to conquer a series of sins. Of particular interest to us is his description of six steps or stages within our souls through which an assailing thought might or might not move from a mere temptation to an actual sin. Here they are in brief:

Saint John Climacus's Stages of the Growth of Sinful Passions
- Provocation
- Coupling
- Assent
- Captivity
- Struggle
- Passion

Provocation is described as a simple word or image that we experience for the first time, and, in the instant that it affects us, is said to enter into our heart. This might be something we encounter out in the world, or a thought or image that intrudes into our awareness out of the blue. Climacus notes that this first stage is *not* sinful.

Coupling is that conversation we have within ourselves regarding that word or image of provocation, with or without passion. This stage *may* be sinful, depending on what we have to say to ourselves and the way we say it.

Assent can be best expressed in the words of Climacus himself: "the delighted yielding of the soul to what it has encountered. ... The condition of the soul determines whether or not the third is sinful."[9] (Note that the scrupulous soul does not typically delight in the scruple — quite the contrary.)

Captivity is "a forcible and unwilling abduction of the heart, a permanent lingering with what we have encountered and which totally undermines the necessary order of our souls." Captivity is judged for its sinfulness in terms of the situation, such as whether it occurs at prayer or at other times, and its subject matter, such as whether it is in regard to something trivial or "in the context of evil thoughts."

Struggle implies the internal struggle against the building attack against the soul, and whether one marshals sufficient power of the soul to counter the attack or succumbs to the pleasures of desire.

Passion is the result of a lost struggle that may remain hidden within the soul but acts to become like a habit — that is, a vice — until the soul clings to it of its own will "with affection." Passion, says Climacus, is always denounced as a sin and calls for either repentance or future punishment.

This sequence rings some bells for me, and perhaps for any of you as well who have grappled with a temptation toward sin and come out as the victor — or loser. Climacus's internal sequence is full of both spiritual and psychological insights. Indeed, we'll refer back to it in our Science of Scrupulosity essays, in which we highlight the best modern psychotherapies for coping with scrupulosity.

Our key focus for now is that first stage of "provocation." The scrupulous are indeed provoked by potentially sinful simple images or words that may seem to enter into our hearts in an instant (akin to *intrusive obsessive thoughts* in psychological terminology). We need to recall that provocations are not sins.

The ancient Stoic philosophers, who sought to foster virtuous behaviors by bringing our emotions under the guidance of reason, took a very similar view. The Roman Seneca (BC 4–AD 65), for example, reported that even a great Stoic sage who had mastered his emotions would experience "proto-passions," or "first movements," the equivalent of Climacus's provocations. We all experience reflexive or automatic bodily reactions to various outside stimuli or even our own thoughts. Who doesn't jump at a loud noise, or get a sinking feeling in our chest if we realize we have forgotten to perform some important task? How many among us can come across a beautiful person of the opposite sex and not be tempted to prolong our glance? Who does not get angry thoughts if someone steps on our toe?

Biological psychologists explain such reactions by the operations of our various layers of brain structures. Lower structures, more akin to those we share with the animals, are set up for quick reflexive responses to things we would hope to avoid or acquire. Only later do our higher brain centers involved in reasoning come on to the scene to evaluate what happened and how we've reacted. We'll examine this in more depth later as well. Again, our lesson here for the scrupulous is to know that "provocations," "proto-passions," "first movements," automatic reactions, reflexive thoughts, fleeting temptations, or base images and intrusive obsessive thoughts that seem to come from nowhere *are not in and of themselves sins.*

We will revisit St. John Climacus's steps when we talk about modern psychotherapies for scrupulosity later in the book. For now, let's conclude our look at sins by a much closer look at that sin that so troubled John Bunyan, and perhaps so many others: that sin of all sins, the sin against the Holy Spirit.

Unforgivable Sins Against the Ever-Merciful Holy Spirit?

I recall during my own 25 years in the desert — not of sand, but of atheism — that philosopher Bertrand Russell, and some other atheists, argued that countless people throughout the ages have suffered for fear that they may have committed the "blasphemy against the Spirit" that God does not forgive (see Mt 12:31–32; Mk 3:28-29; Lk 12:10). Undoubtedly some people have worried about it. Bunyan reported experiencing some partial relief from admitting his fear to another man who told him that he had worried about it too.

We know that Jesus Christ came so that we might have abundant, eternal life with him (see Jn 10:10; 6:40), and that he established, through Peter, a Church on earth to help us get there (Mt 16:18–19). Hence, it should be no surprise that the Church has given us means to know whether or not we have committed special sins against the Holy Spirit. This guidance should offer consolation to all of us, and especially the scrupulous, since these sins are sins that clearly *cannot happen by accident*. In fact, they require considerable and persistent malevolent intention. God's mercy is so great that we must actively work against it if we wish to completely render ourselves, as St. Thomas Aquinas stated in his "Treatise on the Resurrection," "unworthy of His mercy." Sins against the Holy Spirit are briefly addressed in the *Catechism of the Catholic Church* paragraphs 1864, 2091, and 2092. Saint Thomas explains Church teaching on six sins against the Holy Spirit (*ST*, II-II, q.14, a.3). Here they are in brief:

Six Sins Against the Holy Spirit

- **Despair.** This is the complete abandonment of hope in one's salvation through God's goodness, which amounts to the willful denial or rejection of the power of God's mercy.[10] In a poignant passage from the *Dialogues of Saint Catherine of Siena*, God reveals to her that we should never despair of his mercy, regardless of the nature or extent of our sins, if we but turn to him for forgiveness. He tells her that Judas Iscariot's greatest sin was not that he betrayed Jesus Christ, but that he despaired of God's willingness to forgive him even for that.

- **Presumption.** Paragraph 2092 of the *Catechism* tells us that we may commit the sin of presumption either by being overconfident in our own ability to earn salvation without God's help, or by believing that God will grant us our salvation without any effort on our part. As you might surmise, those with scrupulosity rarely struggle with the sin of presumption in its second variety, since they so often worry that their efforts or lack of efforts will deprive them of eternity with God. The scrupulous may well, however, have tendencies toward a variety of the first form of presumption in placing too much trust in their own capacities, their own compulsive rituals to appease God and earn their way to heaven. We would do well to be more willing to submit to the true teaching of the Church on the nature of sin, the means to salvation through the grace of God, and the need to humbly submit to spiritual direction when one's own reason may be disordered.

- **Impugning the known truth.** This means to willfully and actively attack, contradict, distort, or falsify spiritual matters we know to be true. The scrupulous should be aware that this does not mean that one remains in sin against the Holy Spirit if one has worked against the spiritual truths in the past before he knew them to be true, and since repented and changed his ways. Consider, for example, the case of Saul, former persecutor of Christians, now known as Saint Paul.

- **Envy of another's spiritual good.** This is not your ordinary garden-variety envy of someone's new sports car or big house. The opposite of loving charity, this envy begrudges another his hope of happiness and salvation and takes joy in the prospect of his damnation. And the scrupulous should note as well, this does not apply to those among us who in a fit of anger have at one time told another person to "Go to h---!" It is a persistent desire for another's damnation, a desire which one does not attempt to resist and repent of.

- **Obstinacy in sin.** This means stubbornly refusing the power and gifts of the Holy Spirit, and might include willful ignorance of virtue and refusal to fight against our vices. Indeed, it would be hard to label anyone as "willfully ignorant" who desires to read this very chapter against sin, the next two on the virtues, and then the one on the Holy Spirit's gifts!

- **Final impenitence.** A most profoundly grave and sad sin, final impenitence is man's persistent and explicit rejection of God and his mercy. It is a conscious unwillingness to be contrite, to seek out forgiveness, and to have regret, shame, or remorse for our sins. It is certainly not a sin common among the scrupulous. Final impenitence says: "God, I am not sorry for the sins I have committed!" Scrupulosity says, to the contrary: "God, I am sorry for the sins I have committed — and for the possible sins I may or may not have committed!"

- Let's be sure to note well here that final impenitence is the only sin against the Holy Spirit that cannot be forgiven because it is *final,* having occurred at the end of our life with no further opportunities on earth to be repentant. All these other sins, while serious matters, can be forgiven. Indeed, God wants us to repent so that these sins may be forgiven, and so that we can enjoy eternity with him. God's mercy is limitless if we but ask him for it. Many a canonized saint in heaven had committed grave sins at one time, even some sins against the Holy Spirit, before they sought out God's forgiveness and filled their souls with his merciful graces.

Clearly then, such sins are not inadvertent oversights arising through unintended negligence or the temporary insanity of some overriding passion of the moment. They cannot come into or remain in our hearts without our own explicit, willful, and ongoing permission. Those coping with scrupulosity, fearing even minor sins or seeing sins where there are none, are certainly very poor candidates for committing and persisting in sins against the Holy Spirit. If we trust in God's mercy, we need not worry about them.

Let's conclude with the scriptural wisdom of Saint Paul: "Have no anxiety about anything, but in everything by prayer and supplication with thanksgiving let your requests be made known to God. And the peace of God, which passes all understanding, will keep your hearts and your minds in Christ Jesus" (Phil 4:6–7).

Science of Scrupulosity — #1

Help for the Pio(u)s in Measuring Scrupulosity

Are you wondering if you are over scrupulous? Let's look at a questionnaire that modern psychologists have devised to measure tendencies toward scrupulosity: the Pennsylvania Inventory of Scrupulosity-Revised (fittingly known as the PIOS-R!).[11] This is not designed to definitively diagnose scrupulosity as something one does or does not have. There is no cut-off score that lights up and blinks "scrupulosity" if you reach it. Rather, it is a means to look at the likelihood that one is suffering from scrupulosity, and to provide the sufferer (or therapist as the case may be) with insight into the particular characteristics and intensities of one's scrupulous thoughts. If you'd like to give it a try, instructions specify that the listed items simply refer to experiences that people sometimes have. You are to indicate how often you have the experiences in the list using this number key:

0 = never; 1 = almost never; 2 = sometimes; 3 = often; 4 = constantly

1. I worry that I might have dishonest thoughts. 2
2. I fear that I might be an evil person. 2
3. I fear I will act immorally. 2
4. I feel urges to confess sins over and over. 3
5. I worry about heaven and hell. 3
6. I worry I must act morally at all times or I will be punished. 2
7. Feeling guilty interferes with my ability to enjoy things I would like to enjoy. 3
8. Immoral thoughts come into my head, and I can't get rid of them. 2
9. I am afraid my behavior is unacceptable to God. 3

10. I fear I have acted inappropriately without realizing it. 3
11. I must try hard to avoid having certain immoral thoughts. 2
12. I am very worried about things I did that may have been dishonest. 2
13. I am afraid I will disobey God's rules/laws. 3
14. I am afraid of having sexual thoughts. 2
15. I worry I will never have a good relationship with God. 3
16. I feel guilty about immoral thoughts I have had. 3
17. I worry that God is upset with me. 3
18. I am afraid of having immoral thoughts. 2
19. I am afraid my thoughts are unacceptable to God. 3

49

Well, how did you do? If you are troubled with scrupulous thoughts, you might want to jot down the overall score you obtained today. Over time, as you grow in your understanding of scrupulosity and your capacity to cope with it, you may find those numbers declining as you increasingly exchange your feelings of uncertainty and fear with the solace of God's peace.

Saintly Lesson for Scrupulous Souls — #1

St. Ignatius of Loyola (1491–1556)

We should be encouraged to know that a number of canonized saints have struggled with scrupulosity with varying levels of success while living on earth, but all achieved eternal peace in heaven. St. Ignatius of Loyola, founder of the Society of Jesus (the Jesuit order), was among the greatest of those saints who informed us of his scrupulous thoughts and how he overcame them.

Ignatius embraced an adventurous, worldly life as a soldier and ladies man in the kingdom of Castille (now part of Spain). In his mid-twenties, a cannon ball nearly took off both his lower legs. While recovering from the injury, he nourished his mind with books about the lives of the saints, since his sister did not have the books about knightly chivalry that he wanted. Ignatius was deeply moved by the saintly lives, and his heart soon turned to Christ. He sought to do great works of penance to amend for his past life of sin. The saint tells us that he prepared for a general confession by writing down a detailed account of all the past sins he could recall, but after his confession, he was tortured by the idea that he may have left some sins out. After subsequent confessions, he experienced such painful doubts and fears that he even contemplated suicide at times.

Ignatius, however, was not fully bereft of hope. He remained willing to trust in God and to seek out good spiritual direction and counsel. As he put it with such endearing humility: "Show me Lord, where I can obtain help: and if I have to follow a little dog to obtain the cure I need, I am ready to do that."[12] A turning point came one day when a confessor commanded Ignatius never to confess past sins again. Ignatius reported that from that day forward, he trusted in God's mercy and was freed of his scruples.

Father Santa has astutely observed that a key for Saint Ignatius' cure was that "he came to an understanding that scruples are temptations,"[13] as we detailed in some length in this chapter.

When Ignatius's scruples were conquered, he set out to conquer the world for Christ, gathering great saints around him, like Francis Xavier, who would take Christ's Gospel all to the way to India, Japan, and an island off mainland China before he was called to his heavenly home.

The great order founded by Sts. Ignatius of Loyola and Francis Xavier would spread around the world, establishing hundreds of secondary schools and universities in dozens of countries. (One of my own sons went to one — Saint Louis University). Ignatius would also pen the powerful *Spiritual Exercises* that have edified Catholics across the centuries. By obeying his confessor and conquering scrupulosity, Saint Ignatius's focus successfully shifted from despairing over his own temptations to doing everything *ad majorem Dei gloriam*, "for the greater glory of God" — the Jesuit motto. May he inspire us to do the same.

His feast day is July 31. St. Ignatius of Loyola, pray for us so that our trust in God and in our confessor may bring us spiritual peace!

2

Scrupulosity Meets
the Moral Virtues

*Virtue, inasmuch as it is a suitable disposition
of the soul, is like health and beauty, which
are suitable dispositions of the body.*

— St. Thomas Aquinas, *ST*, I-II, q.55, a.2

The gifted spiritual counselor, St. Francis (1567–1622), tells us that sin and anxiety are the soul's greatest enemies: "Anxiety is the soul's greatest enemy, sin only excepted. Therefore, above all else, calm and compose your mind, gently and quietly pursue your aim."[1] Alas, anxiety about sin is the defining characteristic of scrupulosity. And yet, the great saint advises us to overcome these enemies of the soul by calmly composing our minds and proceeding to act in gentleness and quietude.

St. Thomas Aquinas (c. 1225–1274), one of the Church's

greatest theologians, wrote about three stages of spiritual growth in terms of "degrees of charity" (*ST*, II-II, q.24, a.9):

1. Resistance of sin
2. Development of virtue
3. Pursuit of oneness with God

Charity, we are told, increases in a way analogous to growth in human development, from the incapacities of infancy to the manifold powers of maturity. The first degree of charity, akin to our infancy in the spirit, rightly focuses primarily upon the avoidance of sin. While this degree of charity focuses on the *avoidance of evil,* the next degree focuses more clearly on *doing the good*, perhaps the most general "aim" of which Saint Francis speaks.

At the second degree of the development of charity, the pursuit of virtue takes center stage. Here's how Saint Thomas describes it: "In second place, a man's chief pursuit is to aim at progress in good, and this is the pursuit of the proficient, whose chief aim is to strengthen their charity by adding to it." Although pursuing virtue is a noble and efficacious means of squelching sin, those with charity of the second degree must still continue to fight the good fight against their sinful appetites, if and until their attainment of true virtue comes to still this internal discord completely.

As to the third and highest degree, Thomas tells us that, "man's third pursuit is to aim chiefly at union with and enjoyment of God; this belongs to the perfect who desire to be dissolved and to be with Christ." We have a name for people we know have attained this third degree in life — saints! Of course, we are all called to become saints, and those men and women who have been officially recognized and canonized as saints, along with the rest of the vast Communion of Saints of the

Church Triumphant in heaven, have all climbed to the top of the spiritual ladder after starting, like you and me, at the very first rung. Indeed, as we see in our Saintly Lessons on Scrupulosity, many of them started by battling not only sin, but scrupulous fear of sin too.

Now, of special relevance to our focus in this chapter, recall that Thomas said that those with charity of the second degree must still continue their fight against sin until they reach a point that their virtue extinguishes sinful desires. This place with one foot on the second rung of the spiritual ladder is where many of us rest, perhaps for much of our lives. Thomas quite graphically compares our task at this level with the task of those who built the walls of Jerusalem while fighting off their enemies, who "with one hand labored on the work and with the other held his weapon" (Neh 4:17).

In this chapter, we will strive to obtain and employ real spiritual weapons with which to beat down both sin and the fear of sin that is scrupulosity. These psychological and spiritual weapons are the virtues, and rest assured that they are powerful. Indeed, per Saint Thomas, "Virtue denotes a certain perfection of power" (*ST*, I-II, q.71, a.1). And Thomas means that literally too. Look at his quotation where he approvingly echoes Aristotle's observation that virtues are to the soul as health and beauty are to the body. The healthier and fitter we are, the more powerful our bodies are in carrying out activities and in resisting disease. So too, when our souls are at their most powerful, they are in the "most suitable disposition," most ready, willing, and able to make the most of the mental and spiritual capacities God gave us.

We already met one class of virtues that will guide us throughout the rest of this book. The *intellectual virtues* like understanding, science, and wisdom give us power to know the truth, while the *moral virtues* like temperance, fortitude, justice, and prudence give us the power to do the good. As Saint Thomas put it: "For a man to do a good deed, it is requisite that not only his reason be well disposed by means of a habit of intellectual virtue; but also that his appetite be well disposed by a means of a habit of moral virtues" (*ST*, I-II, q.58, a.2). In other words, we need them both, because to do the good, we need to know what is truly good.

Now we will zoom in on the moral virtues, those virtues of doing. These tools for building up our walls of charity may provide us with sharp weapons (or at least hammers and crowbars), for beating down our souls' enemy of scrupulosity while building up virtues within us. Violent metaphors aside, these very same virtuous weapons will serve to gently sooth our souls and calm our minds, since they serve to bring the smoldering desires, passions, imaginings, and anxieties of scrupulosity under the cool control of right reason. Let's begin.

Cardinals Defeat Scruples in Game Seven!

Sorry about that heading, but in these parts (Central Illinois), when it comes to baseball, it is all about the St. Louis Cardinals *or* the Chicago Cubs, with about half the population on either side, and with not a few members of the most loving families split right down the middle! Here though, we'll be talking about some Catholic cardinals, so to speak (but not their Eminences with the scarlet red caps).

Chief among the moral virtues that help us achieve the good are four special virtues of *temperance, fortitude, justice,* and *prudence.* These four are the "cardinal" virtues, the term deriving from the Latin *cardine* for hinge, since the other cardinal virtues essentially hinge on and hang from them. They appear together in Scripture, as for example: "And if any one loves righteousness, her labors are virtues; for she teaches self-control and prudence, justice and courage; nothing in life is more profitable for men than these" (Wis 8:7). Let's begin with a look at all four in brief, before we see how each one can help us fly past scrupulosity.

The Four Cardinal Virtues per St. Thomas Aquinas

VIRTUES	DEFINITION	HUMAN POWERS THEY PERFECT
Temperance	Our capacity to rein in our desires for pleasures.	Concupiscible appetite: Passion to seek what we desire as good.
Fortitude	Our capacity to overcome or endure difficulties to obtain worthwhile goods.	Irascible appetite: Passion to overcome or endure obstacles to our good.
Justice	Our capacity to give to others what is rightfully due to them.	Will, a.k.a. "intellectual appetite": Seeks to obtain good things, overcome/ endure bad things as judged not by passion, but through right reason.
Prudence	Our capacity to determine and perform virtuous means to obtain virtuous goals.	Practical Intellect: Use of reason to determine moral means to attain moral goals.

Tempering Temptation with Temperance

The virtue of temperance gives us the power to rein in our worldly desires when they are excessive or inappropriate. It is aided by virtues focused on particular categories of desire. For example, when St. John Climacus first introduced his six steps of the growth of sinful passions, he did so when discussing the virtue of *chastity* which tempers our sexual desires, since these can be so vehement. Such desires are built upon powerful biological urges which are good when exercised properly. If we develop the virtue of chastity as an aid to temperance, we will be better able to stop illicit sexual thoughts or reactions before they become sinful. As the old television character Deputy Barney Fife would say, the virtue of chastity can help us "Nip it in the bud — Nip-it-in-the-bud!" — that is, before it turns into sin.

Sometimes the scrupulous are disturbed by Jesus' declaration in the Sermon of the Mount that "every one who looks at a woman lustfully has already committed adultery with her in his heart" (Mt 5:28). They should know that an instant reaction of pleasure or attraction to a beautiful person does not in itself constitute a *lustful* look. A mere acknowledgment of a person's physical beauty can be miles away from sin. Indeed, we might even thank God for making such a beautiful creature, bearing in mind that there is also some kind of beauty in every single one of us. If the image or thought does provoke some kind of an instant carnal desire, "entering into the heart," in Climacus's language, it is still but a *provocation* at this point, and develops into sin only if we encourage the thought or image to proceed through the subsequent stages in our minds.

Modern psychologists and philosophers note a strong psychological tendency in those of us who are scrupulous called *moral thought-action fusion,* meaning a failure to distinguish between immoral passing thoughts and actually committing immoral acts, treating immoral thoughts as just as bad (or nearly so) as immoral acts. Per philosophers Summers and Armstrong: "They [the scrupulous] see having unacceptable thoughts, even if they are uncontrollable and intrusive thoughts, as (almost) as bad as having an immoral action (Abramowitz et. al., 2002). The perceived wrongness of having the thought is therefore simply in entertaining its content, however unwillingly."[2]

Examples from the psychological literature, and my own discussions with fellow Catholics, would include sexual thoughts about a person one knows intruding into one's awareness during prayer at home, or even sexual thoughts about a person one happens to see during Mass. We should all be aware that occasional unwanted thoughts such as those are not unusual in and of themselves, and are not sinful in and of themselves, if they arise unwillingly and are not elaborated on purpose, even if it should become difficult to avoid thinking about them. They are not completely unlike the experience most of us have had of not being able to get the lyrics or tune of some song out of our minds at times (even if we find the song most annoying).

Hope for dealing with such thoughts comes from another related virtue that helps temperance rein in all kinds of desires that develop within our souls. St. Thomas Aquinas calls it *continence.* Let's say an unwanted immoral thought intrudes into your awareness in a sacred setting, like at the beginning of Mass. You try not to panic. You tell yourself that this thought is your scrupulosity speaking, and you try to refocus yourself on your prayer. It crops up again a few times, and you strive to ignore it and refocus on the Holy Sacrifice of the Mass. You tell yourself that you did not want this thought, and that you were sincere in reciting the Penitential Rite and you will still go to Communion to receive the healing Body, Blood, Soul, and Divinity of Christ. Perhaps by the end of Mass, you realize that the immoral thought has vanished, at least for now. This kind of internal struggle in which we use our reason (and our trust in God) to rein in an unwanted immoral thought is the virtue of continence in action. Continence refers to the ability to resist evil thoughts within oneself. The continent person struggles within himself against powerful thoughts and desires, and eventually prevails in doing the right thing, though for the scrupulous this may well mean taking the right actions even though doubts or obsessive thoughts have not vanished. In a sense, it is like the person with fortitude (whom we'll meet in our next section), who may still feel fear, but perform a courageous act in spite of it. The truly temperate person, on the contrary, has trained himself to the point that he no longer feels the pull of strong and vehement immoral desires.

If, through repeated struggles and successes, the immoral thoughts or desires have vanished, or at least can be easily ignored, full-blown temperance has arrived on the scene. Through repeated acts of the virtue of continence is the virtue of temperance built. Indeed, while it may seem difficult for some people even to begin to enter the fray against immoral thoughts, some successful methods of therapy we'll address in these pages (such as Exposure and Response Prevention Therapy) can be seen as specific methods one can use to build up one's continence, and perhaps, for some, to arrive someday at pure temperance.

Yet there are still more helpful tricks up temperance's sleeve, so to speak. Let's listen first to how St. Julian of Norwich (1343–after 1416) describes it in reference to people with scrupulosity: "When they begin to hate sin and amend themselves according to the laws of the Holy Church, still there persists a fear that moves them to look at themselves and their sins in the past. And they take this fear for humility, but it is a reprehensible blindness and weakness."[3]

The key words here are "fear" and "humility," which this great female saint tells us should never be confused. St. Thomas Aquinas addresses the virtue of humility in the context of virtues that assist temperance. How so? Well, temperance reins in not only carnal or bodily desires, but any kind of desires: "to temper and restrain the mind, lest it tend to high things immoderately; and this belongs to the virtue of humility" (*ST*, II-II, q.161, a.1). As we read in Scripture: "Seek not what is too difficult for you" (Sir 3:21), and "Do not lift a weight beyond your strength" (Sir 13:2). True humility does recall that we are like *humus* (from the earth) and have fallen sinful natures, but it does not forget the power of God's forgiveness and the fact that while we can do little on our own, in the words of Saint Paul, "I can do all things in him who strengthens me" (Phil 4:13). Note that Saint Julian calls fear, but not humility, a "weakness." Indeed, as every weightlifter knows, a weight that you might not budge at the start of your training may seem like child's play someday down the road. What is too difficult for us today may not be tomorrow, if we cooperate with God's grace.

When God forgives our sins, he certainly does not want us to perpetually relive and wallow in them. Rather, he has important things for all of us to do. He does not want us to cower in fear and remorse. That is not humility. Let's listen to Saint Thomas once more: "It is contrary to humility to aim at greater things through confiding in one's own powers: but to aim at greater things through confidence in God's help, is not contrary to humility; especially since the more one subjects oneself to God, the more one is exalted in God's sight" (*ST*, II–II, q.161, a.1). It is scrupulous fear, and not the lowly yet powerful virtue of humility, that thinks God would rather cast us down for our potential for sin than exalt us for our potential for virtue.

Fortitude Fights Fears

While temperance harnesses our concupiscible appetite through which we seek out things that we love, fortitude (from the Latin *fortis* for strength) employs our *irascible* appetite through which we raise our ire, so to speak, to overcome or endure difficult obstacles that keep us from the truly good things we love. Its most common synonym is courage (from the Latin *cor* for heart) and the scrupulous would do well to strive to grow in this virtue, for the scrupulous sincerely desire God and the chance to abide with him in eternity, but scrupulosity itself would seem to present an imposing obstacle in their way.

Well, fear is a key component of scrupulosity — fear of sin, that is — and fortitude's main job is to overcome or endure fears of great obstacles along our path to heaven. We should all be well aware that, through fortitude and trust in God, some great saints and many everyday Catholics have indeed been able to *overcome* scrupulosity, as we saw with St. Ignatius of Loyola. Some priests in our own day speak of parishioners they have worked with who report having been cured of their scrupulosity.

How does one know when one has been cured? In a nutshell, per Fr. Kaler, CCSR, "when they can distinguish between a temptation and a sin and not worry about confession, Communion, and already forgiven sins, they're cured."[4]

Other people battling against scrupulosity may never be completely "cured," but can attain greater peace and still live holy, happy lives, and even become great saints and Doctors of the Church! Indeed, we will meet one of the greatest patron saints of scrupulosity in this chapter's Saintly Lessons for Scrupulous Souls.

Fortitude also comes to the aid and serves as a bulwark for those who may never completely overcome some scrupulous tendencies. While fortitude helps us overcome some obstacles, per St. Thomas Aquinas, "the principal act of fortitude is endurance, that is to stand immobile in the face of dangers rather than attack them" (*ST*, II-II, q.123. a.6). If we apply this idea to the treatment of scrupulosity, Saint Thomas, as he so often does, shows amazing insight and foresight. In Science of Scrupulosity

#4, when we examine Exposure and Response Prevention — the present-day gold standard psychological treatment for scrupulosity — we will find that the fundamental principle behind it is to calmly endure, to mentally "stand immobile," so to speak, in the face of one's own scrupulous thoughts.

Doing Justice to One's Own Soul

St. Thomas Aquinas defines the virtue of *justice* as giving another his or her rightful due. Rather than reining in or firing up lower appetites, justice operates according to the guidance of the human will as directed by reason, the will being also called the intellectual appetite. At the most fundamental level, justice entails doing the good and not doing evil to others. Broad categories of justice that Thomas calls its "subjective parts" include *distributive justice,* which, akin to what we speak of today as "social justice," refers to the way in which a community (or nation or organization of any kind) distributes common goods to each individual. The other subjective part is *commutative justice,* and this regards the relation of one part to another. It refers to private individuals and the mutual dealings between them. Per our *Catechism,* "Without commutative justice, no other form of justice is possible" (2411). In other words, all justice must begin at home, in the way we treat others in our daily lives.

Thomas also elucidates a variety of related virtues that serve justice for particular objects and circumstances.

First among these is the virtue of **religion** itself, which is directed toward what we owe to God. Thomas notes, perhaps surprisingly, that religion "falls short" of the cardinal virtue of justice. With God as its object, how can that be? Well, the complete definition of justice is to give to another their rightful due "in equal measure." Religion falls short of justice only in the fact that we can never give back in equal measure what God has given to us! The very fact that we exist in the world, that there is even a world in which to exist, and that we have a heaven to look forward to, is all due to the unbounded generosity of God. We can never pay him back in equal measure and — please take note — he certainly knows that and does not expect us to! He only expects us to love him and cooperate with his grace as fallen, fallible women and men. We exercise the virtue of religion through internal acts like devotion and prayer and external acts like adoration, sacrifices, oblations[5] and firstfruits,[6] tithes, oaths, and vows. Unfortunately, virtually all of these activities can become the subject matter for needless scruples, but we'll try to do them justice in upcoming chapters.

A second virtue serving justice is **piety**, which requires that we give special deference and respect to our parents and to our nation, since they too gave us things that we can never fully repay in equal measure. As Thomas puts it so clearly: "Man is debtor chiefly to his parents and his country, after God" (*ST*, II-II, q.101, a.1). The fourth commandment — "Honor your father and your mother" — is a commandment of piety. Unfortunately, piety can be so prone to misunderstanding that the first psychological scale to measure scrupulosity is, as we've seen, known as the PIOS. We'll clear things up further when we get to chapter 4 and examine not only the virtue, but the Holy Spirit's gift of piety.

Observance is another special virtue in service of justice. It has two key components. *Dulia* means honor or respect for another person's excellence. I happen to live in Springfield, Illinois, where *dulia* is seen all over the place, with our airport and a great variety of things named after our most honored son, a man of great social and individual justice: Abraham Lincoln.

And speaking of justice, I happen to be writing today on January 17, 2022, a date that honors another great American champion of justice, Dr. Martin Luther King, Jr. No stranger himself to the writings of Aquinas, King would write in his Letter from a

Birmingham Jail: "To put it in the terms of Saint Thomas Aquinas: An unjust law is a human law that is not rooted in eternal law and natural law. Any law that uplifts human personality is just. Any law that degrades human personality is unjust."[7]

Of course, every Catholic should remember that we owe some sense of *dulia* to every single person we meet. Saint Paul told us as much: "In humility count others better than yourselves. Let each of you look not only to his own interests, but also to the interests of others" (Phil 2:3–4). Of special importance to every personal struggle with scrupulosity is the *dulia* owed to one's confessor or spiritual adviser. We'll dig into this more deeply in chapter 5 on the sacraments.

Following right along with this idea, the second key component to the virtue of observance is the virtue of *obedience.* We will begin to dig into this one when we contemplate the advice of St. Alphonsus Liguori at this chapter's end.

Liberality derives from the Latin word *liber*, meaning "free," and is the virtue of free and generous giving. Saint Thomas notes that "justice gives another what is his, whereas liberality gives another what is one's own." Further, justice considers "the legal due," while liberality "considers a certain moral due." Liberality then is a generosity beyond the call of legal duty and of nature. As Thomas puts it so well, "to spend on oneself is an inclination of nature; hence to spend money on others belongs properly to a virtue" (*ST*, II-II, q.117, a.5).

A potential pitfall for those of us prone to scruples is to think that we must extend this virtue beyond its golden mean, so to speak, being forever fearful that we are too selfish and are not giving enough to the Church or other charitable causes. All of us should note very well that liberality does not imply recklessness in our giving. Thomas uses an apt military metaphor here, noting that a virtuous soldier's fortitude consists not only in wielding his sword in battle, but in sharpening it in between battles and storing it in its sheath. So too liberality means not only giving away money, but always using reasonable means to earn money and save some back, so that it can be employed when and where it is truly most needed.

Affability or friendliness is something we owe to every single human being we meet. Not everyone can become a close friend, but because of our social nature we derive joy from each other's company and we owe it to one another not to rob them of their joy through our rudeness, neglect, or disrespect. Indeed, "a certain natural equity obliges a man to live agreeably with his fellow-men; unless some reason should oblige him to sadden them for their good" (*ST*, II-II, q.114, a.2). Such affability can be displayed by actions as simple as a brief hello or a simple acknowledging nod and a smile to a stranger we happen to pass.

People with scrupulosity do not tend to lack in affability. Most are friendly folks. In fact, some people with scrupulous tendencies will ruminate over encounters with others, entertaining obsessive thoughts about the possibility that maybe they inadvertently said or did something offensive. They may also dread facing certain social occasions out of fear that they may do so. Still, the scrupulous need not worry that they've sinned against the virtue of affability unless they've *intentionally* done so. Further, on some occasions, if the scrupulous should irritate someone by going on and on about scrupulous worries, they should be aware that that other person may indeed feel the need to "sadden them for their good," by asking them to stop talking about their worries. In such cases, the friendliest thing to do would be to take that person's unwanted, but friendly advice!

Gratitude is what we owe to all who have provided us any kind of benefit. It is a joyful acknowledgment and feeling of thanks that vibrantly colors our thoughts, words, and deeds. Saint Paul counseled long ago, "Give thanks in all circumstances; for this is the will of God in Christ Jesus for you" (1 Thes 5:18). At the same time Saint Paul was crafting his letters, the Roman philosopher Lucius Annaeus Seneca (BC 4–AD 65) was writing an entire book on the nature and benefits of gratitude: *De Beneficiis,* "On Benefits." Thirteen centuries, later when St. Thomas Aquinas wrote his masterful analysis of gratitude as a virtue serving justice, he borrowed heavily from the Stoic Seneca while fleshing out his philosophical lessons with truths from Christ and his Church (*ST*, II-II, q. 106). Moving another eight centuries ahead to our own time, the scientific field of cognitive psychotherapy itself has been awakened to the power of inculcating an attitude of gratitude as a means of attaining better mental health.[8]

For now, the scrupulous may want to look back again at the quotation from Saint Paul. If you want to follow God's will, do not forget that he wants you to be thankful, not fearful. This is why Jesus Christ suffered for you. Thanks be to God!

We owe each other the **truth**. No one wants to be lied to, and God has instructed us in the eighth commandment not to bear false witness against our neighbor. What we believe should correspond to what we say. To tell the truth is a good act. To develop within ourselves the habit of telling the truth, then, is a virtue essential to justice.

This virtue may become distorted among some scrupulous souls by excessive worries over minor "fibs" or "white lies" at most, or slight exaggerations at least, uttered precisely out of respect for the virtue of affability! When great aunt Ethel asks how we liked her famous, and usually delicious casserole, very few among us would tell her it almost made us gag because she apparently forgot that she added one of the spices and must have added it again a time or two. Indeed, there are subtler ways to get the message across. When I ask my wife how she likes some new concoction I whipped up, I can usually sense that I've missed the mark when she simply responds with a noncommittal, "Uh-huh."

So, the scrupulous do indeed tend to value the virtue of

truth, but may worry that they have transgressed through the most minor words. There is another sense though, in which the scrupulous among us can benefit from a deeper dive into the virtue of truth. Let's reexamine our guiding quotation from Pope St. John Paul II, moving our emphasis to the last half of the quotation (italics added): "Faith and reason are like two wings on which the human spirit rises to the contemplation of truth; and God has placed in the human heart a desire to know truth — *in a word, to know himself — so that, by knowing and loving God, men and women may also come to the fulness of truth about themselves.*"

Saint Thomas tells us that, strictly speaking, all justice is social "since justice by its name implies equality, it denotes essentially relation to another, for a thing is equal, not to itself, but to another" (*ST*, II-II, q.58, a.2). Now, if you can remember back that far, our section on justice started with the heading, "Doing Justice to One's Own Soul." So how does that jibe with the wisdom of the Angelic Doctor? Well, Thomas notes that we can also speak of a *metaphorical justice* which refers to treating one person's principles of action, such as reason and the concupiscible and irascible appetites, as if they were agents of action themselves. Thus, metaphorically speaking, we can say that in the just person, the appetites and emotions obey the commands of reason, rendering reason its rightful due.

So, some of us might get into the habit of doing our intellectual powers of reasoning "justice," so to speak, by recognizing and acknowledging that the scrupulous doubts that pop into our heads are really our irrational passions and fears speaking, and we need to give our power of reason its own turn to speak as well. A former American presidential candidate once famously quipped to a debate opponent whom he claimed was making erroneous statements, "There you go again!" If we catch ourselves in a scrupulous thought and can say to ourselves, "There *I* go again!" we are both moving toward a greater understanding of ourselves, and doing justice to the God-given powers of our rational soul. It will behoove those battling scrupulosity to come to a deeper understanding of the fulness of truth about themselves, a la John Paul II, by rendering reason its rightful due, à la St. Thomas Aquinas. In fact, the job of the fourth cardinal virtue to which we now turn is to bring our appetites, our thoughts, our emotions, and our actions under the watchful guard of right reason.

Prudence Prevails Over Scrupulosity

Fortitude has been called the "guardian of the virtues," since it keeps us focused on virtue even when the going gets tough. *Prudence,* our final cardinal virtue, has been called the *auriga virtutum,* "charioteer of the virtues" (CCC 1806), because of its guiding function. Also called "practical wisdom," prudence is both an intellectual and a moral virtue. In brief, per Saint Thomas, (echoing Aristotle), "prudence is right reason applied to action" (*ST,* II-II, q.47, a.2, a.6, a.8).

The virtue of prudence and the powers of reason are of vital importance in the development of scrupulosity, and in its cure. Dr. Ciarrochhi usefully distinguished between *developmental scrupulosity* and *emotional scrupulosity*, noting that "the word developmental implies a stage people pass through," though "scruples are not limited to any particular phase."[9]

Philosophers have been aware of human developmental stages for millennia. In the time of Aristotle in the fourth century BC, the child's reasoning capacities were believed to blossom at around the age of 7, when primary educational studies were to begin. Secondary studies would commence at around the age of 14. Sixteen centuries later, the developmental psychologist Jean Piaget would define a stage of "concrete operational" reasoning capacities as blossoming around age 7 and higher, abstract "formal operational" reasoning capacities beginning for most children around the age of 12. Among the newly blossoming powers of late childhood and early adolescence are "hypothetical reasoning" or if-then thinking capacities.

Dr. Ciarrochi notes that the first situation that tends to trigger *developmental scrupulosity* is the advent of adolescence. Some adolescents who are serious about religion will become inspired to give themselves to God. Indeed, I recall a time myself, during a high school religion class, when I thought to myself, "*If* all this stuff we've been taught about God is true, *then* this is the most important stuff in the world, and I should seriously try to live my life according to it." A subset of such adolescents, especially those with "tender consciences" sensitive to moral or ethical issues, will come to focus excessively upon sin. Dr. Ciarrochi gives the example of a fifteen-year-old boy who became so obsessed with the plight of the starving in Africa that he nearly starved himself and gave his allowance for a food relief program in Africa. Not only that, but he would harangue his younger siblings whenever they wasted any food, sometimes sending them away from the table crying.

Perhaps some of us can think of excessive moral crusades we went on during adolescence only to later realize our misguided zeal as we continued to mature and to grow in our faith. Many people with episodes of scruples in adolescence do go on to outgrow them. Another kind of developmental scruple develops in adulthood in the context of a deep religious conversion, as we saw in the case of St. Ignatius of Loyola.

Dr. Ciarrocchi contrasts developmental scrupulosity that a person usually outgrows with longer lasting emotional scrupulosity, the kind that may meet some or all of the criteria for obsessive-compulsive disorder. We'll investigate these criteria in this chapter's Science of Scrupulosity essay. People with emotional scrupulosity have a difficult time employing prudence to guide their own chariots in accord with right reason. A greater understanding of just what prudence is might help to shift their chariots in the right direction.

St. Thomas Aquinas, as you might surmise by now, has examined the virtue of prudence in unparalleled depth. He started with the insights of the Roman philosopher Cicero (BC 106–43), echoed by his own teacher, St. Albert the Great (c. 1200–1280), describing three main "parts" of the virtue of prudence: *memory, understanding,* and *foresight.* These also highlight how prudence relates to the past, the present, and the future. To set and achieve virtuous goals in the future (foresight), requires that we act in the present (understanding current situations), guided by what we have learned in the past (stored in our memories). Interestingly and helpfully, some ancient artistic personifications of prudence depicted a woman with three faces — one each to look at the past, present, and future! Remember that image. We'll be back to it soon.

Good Saint Thomas took those insights from Cicero and Albert and fleshed them out in greater detail, borrowing insights from other philosophers, including Aristotle and Macrobius (AD 370–430), yielding a full eight "parts," or allied capacities and virtues, required to exercise prudence in its fullest. Let's inventory all these parts one by one, and see how they might be used to replace damaged or worn-out parts within the minds and souls of the scrupulous.

Saint Thomas, following his great teacher, Saint Albert, taught that **memory** is not just something we are born with, but a mental and moral potential we can develop through proper training. I can't help but mention that memory training was my own specialty area in psychology, and I've written books about just what these two great saints were talking about,[10] but we need not go there in depth as our focus is on scrupulosity.

If you'll recall our image of three-faced Lady Prudence, a common problem among the scrupulous is that they get too fixated on the face that peers into the past. The scrupulous need to become able to better employ their present- and future-looking faces, rather than peering backward at past sins that God has already forgiven. They should bear in mind as well, that God has given us potentially limitless capacities in our long-term memories, and this is a good thing. Indeed, Saint Augustine said that it is through our capacities of understanding, will, and memory that we mirror the Holy Trinity! The memories of past sins may always be with us and may come to conscious awareness at times. Certain places, people, or situations may spontaneously trigger them, but unless we choose to entertain and relish such recollections, spontaneous memories of past sins are not new sins!

Understanding in the context of prudence refers to the capacity to apply universal moral principles we have grasped to particular situations. In terms of scrupulosity, this could mean striving to apply what the Church actually teaches about the nature of sin, and especially mortal sins, to particular behaviors one is worrying about. If the behavior does not meet the criteria — that is, grave matter, full knowledge, and deliberate consent in the case of mortal sins — prudence would dictate one's worrying must cease.

Docility is the willingness to be taught by others. Thomas explains in quaint and touching language that "in matters of prudence, man stands in very great need of being taught by others, especially by old folk who have acquired a sane understanding of the ends in practical matters" (*ST*, II-II, q.49, a.3). Those "old folks" in our day may literally be older people, like our own folks who have our best interest in minds. Of course, for people of any age battling serious scruples, they may be in greatest need of learning from their priests, confessors, spiritual directors, and possibly counselors or psychotherapists.

In a real sense, docility may be the most crucial of prudence's parts for those with serious emotional scrupulosity, working hand-in-hand with the virtue of obedience. The truly saintly expert on scrupulosity from the inside out, St. Alphonsus Liguori, could hardly make the point more forcefully (and you should forgive the harsh language by remembering that he was including himself): "When doubts and scruples of conscience assail you, you yourself are ignorant, unbalanced, and incapable of forming a judgement. Believe that. … Possibly you will have to put up with the fears that torment you until you die. There is only one course of action — go ahead in blind obedience."[11] If scrupulosity has rendered you, at this time, unable to think and act prudently about particular religious matters, then you should defer with docility to the prudence of a wise confessor or spiritual director, until your own prudence is back on its feet.

And as for a spiritual director, to adapt an old popular song lyric: "You better *not* shop around!" Scrupulous people in the know have remarked on the tendency toward "shopping around" from priest to priest, doubting the advice of the first one … or two … or three. It is best to use but one spiritual director and to do what he says. St. Alphonsus Liguori advises us to choose one director and do what he says. If your director leads you wrong, you are not culpable!

Reason refers to the ability to get at truths by step-by-step rational processes, starting with the information we glean from our senses, as opposed to the kind of direct intuition possessed by the angels who are purely spiritual beings. People battling scrupulosity are just as capable of reasoning as everyone else. Many are highly intelligent in very many ways. But in regards to the subject matter of their scruples, even while they may realize at some level that their scrupulous fears are irrational, they find themselves unable to bring their emotions under the control of right reason, and are therefore unable to act prudently regarding their obsessions and compulsions.

The proper use of reason to guide our emotions and behaviors is a cornerstone of the kinds of cognitive therapies for
scrupulosity we'll describe in subsequent Science of Scrupulosity essays. Even the current name of the earliest of the cognitive
therapies from the 1950s — psychologist Albert Ellis's Rational
Emotive Behavior Therapy — starts with an adjectival form of
the word *reason.* The goal of the psychological and spiritual remedies we'll apply will be to put reason back in the driver's seat
so one's doubts, uncertainties, worries, and fears will once again
have to answer to reason or get out of the car.

Foresight is that forward-looking face so integral to, and almost synonymous with, prudence. Since prudence seeks present
means to future ends or goals, we need the capacity to predict
the future impact of the means we choose to employ. Thomas
cites Saint Isidore, who wrote that "a prudent man is one who
sees from afar (*porro videns*): and this is also the derivation from
providentia (foresight) according to Boethius" (*ST*, II-II, q.49,
a.6). Even individuals with serious scruples will often have the
foresight to predict that their suffering is unlikely to get any better unless they trust in God and are willing to take actions to
conquer their scruples, or at least to better endure them.

Caution: We've all heard the saying that "fools rush in
where angels fear to tread."[12] Well, prudence is the opposite of
foolishness, so prudent souls are also sure, if you'll pardon the
use of another even older old saying, to "look before they leap."[13]
Saint Thomas explained, well before either slogan came about,
that sometimes "evil has the appearance of good. Wherefore,
prudence needs caution, so that we may have such a grasp of
good as to avoid evil" (*ST*, II-II. q.49, a.8). In regards to the scrupulous, we must recall once more the nature of virtues as "golden
means." One can fall short of the mean through a vice of *deficien-
cy* — like fools lacking caution who don't hesitate to jump when
they shouldn't — or one can overshoot the mean through a vice

of *excess* — like some scrupulous people who tend to stay frozen in uncertainty, unable to jump when they should out of an excessive caution produced not by prudence, but by uncertainty and fear. Again, a goal for the scrupulous is to be able to come to give caution its rightful due, but not more than is needed.

Further, while such a careful application of caution was needed in Thomas's thirteenth century, it may be all the more necessary in our modern culture, when so many young people, and even not so young people, seem overly cautious, finding it harder than ever to commit to things like a work vocation or a marital relationship. The scrupulous person seeks a certainty that scruples themselves prevent. The scrupulous among us would do well to keep in mind that God grants us the will and the freedom to make choices of our own, sometimes even between two goods. God essentially asks us, "What do *you* want?" and is happy to trust in our prudence to give it our best shot![14]

Circumspection means seeing "all around" an issue, considering which particular courses of action are likely to be the best in complex situations. On rare occasions, circumspection will lead prudent souls to decide that in certain cases, behaviors that are usually most appropriate should not be performed. Thomas provides an interesting example: "Thus to show signs of love to someone seems, considered in itself, to be a fitting way to arouse love in his heart, yet if pride or suspicion of flattery arise in his heart, it will no longer be a means suitable to the end" (*ST*, II-II, q.49, a.7). Still, in issues touching on their scruples, scrupulous souls could be said to exercise not circumspection, but circum*speck*tion, so to speak, focusing not on relevant circumstances that make a moral difference, but on irrelevant "specks." A popular idiom today for this is "sweating the small stuff." We'll look more at this idea, including the issue of literal material specks, when we address scrupulosity and the sacraments.

Shrewdness: I do not know about you, but lately when I've looked around for certain products or parts, I'm finding them out of stock and on back order. Well, I'm addressing this component of prudence last, because for the scrupulous, in matters bearing on their scrupulosity, shrewdness may be the hardest part of prudence to acquire — but if they put their order in now, it will hopefully someday arrive at their soul's door.

So, what did Thomas mean by shrewdness in relation to the virtue of prudence? He answers this question in a nutshell, by contrasting it with docility: "Now just as docility consists in a man being well disposed to acquire a right opinion from another man, so shrewdness is an apt disposition to acquire a right estimate by oneself" (*ST*, II-II, q.49. a.4). And, of course, Thomas uses man to speak of humanity as a whole. It works just the same way in women!

In other words, shrewdness is the capacity to make quick moral decisions on courses of action when there is no time to deliberate or seek guidance from others. It is the ability to think on one's feet, and then act promptly on what one has decided. In some sense, shrewdness is the opposite of scrupulosity. While scrupulosity hesitates, doubts, questions, and seeks reassurances, shrewdness quickly decides what to do and then does it. Cognitive psychotherapists speak of "automatic thoughts" that tend to pop into our heads without apparent prompting. The kind of automatic thoughts produced by scrupulosity lead to hesitance, doubt, and a reluctance to exercise one's own prudence. The kind of automatic thoughts that are nurtured by proper psychological and spiritual guidance may one day come to replace them, rendering the once scrupulous now shrewd and prudent.

Let's end this chapter with a little recap of the right reason of prudence's parts and how they relate to the less-than-perfect reason of scrupulosity.

How to Keep the Eight Parts of Prudence in Stock

PRUDENCE'S PARTS	ORDERING INSTRUCTIONS
Memory	Remember the distinction between temptation and true sin. Remember to heed the instructions of trusted counselors and/or confessors. Remember that spontaneously remembering past sins is not sinful in itself.
Understanding	Seek a better grasp of the true teachings of the Church so you will be less likely to see sin where there is none.
Docility	In matters related to your scruples, be willing to learn from others like your counselor or priest, and submit in obedience to the guidance of your confessor or spiritual director, delaying exercise of your own prudence until you have built it up.
Reason	Realize that God gave you reason, intellect, and will for very good reasons, and with continued prayer and work you will improve your capacity to bring your fears under your reason's control.

PRUDENCE'S PARTS	ORDERING INSTRUCTIONS
Foresight	Look ahead to the negative consequences if you do nothing about your scruples, but more so to the positive consequences for you and your loved ones if you continue to fight the good fight to put scrupulosity in its place.
Caution	You may already have too much of this one in stock! Make sure you are not overly cautious. Be willing to make leaps, even if you *feel* uncertain, if you know that what you're doing does not contradict Church teaching.
Circumspection	This one may be overstocked too! Don't confuse a reasonable circumspection with a circum*speck*tion that is always sweating the small stuff.
Shrewdness	Look forward to ordering and enjoying this part one day, after the other parts have come in and you've tried them and found them in good working order. At that point you may find yourself well-stocked in prudence, and almost out of scruples.

Science of Scrupulosity — #2

Understanding Obsessive-Compulsive Disorder (OCD)

Therapists often fail in their treatment of OCD, not because of deficiencies in their therapy skills, but due to an insufficient understanding of the disorder.

David A. Clark, Ph.D.[15]

Scrupulosity for some people may rise to the level of obsessive-compulsive disorder, either on its own or in combination with obsessions and compulsions regarding non-religious issues too — things like cleanliness or order, for examples.

In previous editions of the Diagnostic and Statistical Manual (DSM) of the American Psychiatric Association, OCD was classed among other disorders featuring anxiety, though now (in the current DSM-5-TR) it is placed in its own class along with "related disorders" that include such things as trichotillomania (compulsive hair-pulling) and hoarding. Its main diagnostic criteria remain mostly the same. Here they are for the "obsessive" half of the diagnosis:

1. Recurrent and persistent thoughts, urges, or images that are experienced, at some time during the disturbance, as intrusive, unwanted, and that in most individuals cause marked anxiety or distress.
2. The individual attempts to ignore or suppress such thoughts, urges, or images, or to neutralize them with some thought or action (i.e., by performing a compulsion).

So, some kind of supposedly immoral thought or image gives rise to some kind of compensatory, anxiety-reducing behavior, like repetitive prayer or seeking reassurance from others, for examples. Note too that, in order to classify as a mental disorder, such thoughts must occur often, last a long time, and cause the sufferer significant distress. But still more is required for a person's scrupulosity to rise to the level of OCD. Here are the criteria regarding the performance of a *compulsion:*

1. Repetitive behaviors (e.g., hand washing, ordering, checking) or mental acts (e.g., praying, counting, repeating words silently) that the person feels driven to perform in response to an obsession, or according to the rules that must be applied rigidly.
2. The behaviors or mental acts are aimed at preventing or reducing distress or preventing some dreaded event or situation. However, these behaviors or mental acts are either not connected in a realistic way with what they are designed to neutralize or prevent or are clearly excessive.

The person with repugnant thoughts (in our case, scrupulous thoughts regarding sin) feels she *must* perform some kind of behavior to counteract the anxiety she feels from the scrupulous thought. Further, these compensatory behaviors must be performed just right, according to the standards that she creates. While these compulsive behaviors are performed to reduce stress and anxiety, they have no real connection with the obsessive thoughts, and they are carried out in an extreme manner. (Any Catholic might cross himself, ask God's forgiveness, or say a quick Act of Contrition if he realizes he has lingered on an immoral thought, but the scrupulous may decide he needs to say a specific number of elaborate prayers in response to even a fleeting immoral image — and start all over again if he loses track of this thoughts while praying.)

There is more still to actual OCD:

The obsessions and compulsions cause marked distress, are time consuming (take more than one hour a day), *or* significantly interfere with the person's normal routine, occupational or academic functioning, or usual social activities or relationships.

In addition, there are "rule-out" criteria. For example, if a person already meets the criteria for another psychiatric disorder that can give rise to obsessions and compulsions — like substance addiction where the person may ruminate about obtaining drugs, or major depression where a person may ruminate over guilty thoughts — and their obsessions and compulsions regard only issues related to that disorder, one would *not* diagnose OCD along with it. Furthermore, the disturbance must not be due to the direct physiological effects of a substance (e.g., drug abuse, a medication) or a general medical condition.

The diagnosing mental health professional is also asked to designate the person's degree of *insight* into their problem as follows:

- With good or fair insight: The individual recognizes that obsessive-compulsive beliefs are definitely or probably not true, or that they may or may not be true.
- With poor insight: The individual thinks obsessive-compulsive disorder beliefs are probably true.
- With absent insight/delusional beliefs: The individual is completely convinced that obsessive-compulsive disorder beliefs are true.

Finally, the clinician is asked to designate if the individual has a current or past history of a tic disorder, a history of uncontrollable twitches, blinks, or verbal outbursts (though well less than 1 percent of children and ½ percent of adults do).

Note well that I have not provided these criteria so that I can diagnose you or so you can diagnose yourself, but so that if you wonder if you or a loved one suffer from scrupulosity to the extent that it is a subtype of the psychiatric impairment of obsessive-compulsive disorder, this might help you determine if you (or he or she) might want to consider seeking help from a mental health professional. But there is still so much more to understanding scrupulosity, so let's continue, shall we?

Scrupulosity, in its more serious forms, may constitute but one subtype of a number of kinds of obsessive-compulsive disorders that may center on a variety of different issues, including for example, the compulsive fear of contamination and the compulsive need for hand-washing or housecleaning, or the extreme need for symmetry and order. In my younger years while working at a state inpatient mental health center, I recall the case of a very ill young man with a variety of impairments, including schizophrenia. The staff observed that he took exceedingly long showers, and after a time came to learn that he had a cleaning ritual in which he had to lather and scrub each body part a specific number of times in a specific order, and if he lost track, he'd start all over again. Further, this same young man walked in straight lines and made 90 degree turns to the left or right, suffering from both contamination and symmetry-order obsessions and compulsions.

Though his case was extreme, I wonder if it might strike any chords in other ways for many of us? A common somewhat obsessive-compulsive pattern regards checking on things like locking doors, shutting garage doors, turning off the oven, etc. Indeed, I'll admit that a time or two when I've headed off to the gym, lost in thought in the wee hours of the morning, I've turned around a few blocks down the road to make sure the garage door was shut, since my wife was asleep in the house. I remember once as a child, spinning around time and again in a chair, and thinking that perhaps I should spin the same number of times in the other direction to even things out. I even remember thinking that God must know the exact number of spins I'd need to do! It never became a pattern (thank God!), but I can still remember the thought. Have you ever had thoughts like these in your past? Many of us have at one time or another. In fact, various studies over the last several decades estimate that around 90 percent of us have at times!

As for recurring, distressing obsessions and compulsions that would indicate an obsessive-compulsive disorder, thankfully this applies to only about 2.3% of Americans throughout their lifetimes.[16] Per the DSM-5-TR, the average age of onset in the United States and several other countries is about 19.5 years. Women are slightly more likely to be diagnosed with OCD in adulthood, while men are more likely to be diagnosed in childhood. For now, though, I'll note that *scrupulosity* in particular may exist as one anxious member of a tightly strung family of obsessive disorders, but it certainly has its unique individuality too. We'll dig deeper into all this in the Science of Scrupulosity at the end of our next chapter.

Saintly Lesson for Scrupulous Souls — #2

St. Alphonsus Liguori (1696–1787)

Alphonsus Liguori struggled with scrupulosity for most his life on earth, yet he became a lawyer and then a priest; founded a religious order (the Congregation of the Most Holy Redeemer, commonly known as the Redemptorists); became a profound and prolific theologian, Mariologist, and Doctor of the Church;[17] and now smiles down upon us from heaven.

Alphonsus, born in Naples, Italy, was the oldest of eight children. Fr. Santa, himself a spiritual son of Saint Alphonsus as a Redemptorist, notes that Alphonsus was reportedly very close to his mother, who had a "tender conscience" and perhaps scrupulosity. Young Alphonsus struggled with scruples so frequently that he became somewhat of a confessor-shopper. Indeed, "he exhausted most of the confessors in Naples trying to come to a decision with certitude."[18]

This great saint once concluded with powerful insight from his insider's perspective, "Scruples are useful in the beginning of conversion. … They cleanse the soul, and at the same time make it careful."[19] As we will examine in more depth in chapter 4 on the Holy Spirit's gifts, a fear of the Lord that dreads sin can be our first step up the spiritual ladder toward heaven. Further, as the lessons in this chapter suggest, battling against scruples can exercise our fortitude and make us stronger in the long haul.

Our great saint was also known for his loving devotion to the Blessed Mother, which no doubt enabled him to persevere and achieve great things by strengthening him in his battle against scruples. In his poignant "On the Seventh Dolor. The Burial of the Body of Jesus," within his book *The Glories of Mary,* Alphonsus relates the story of a religious almost driven to despair by scruples who achieved great comfort by contemplating the *do-*

lors (mental anguish or grief) of Mary. At his time of death, the devil appeared to torment him with scruples, and the Blessed Mother appeared to him and said:

> "And why, oh my son, art thou so overcome with sorrow, thou who has so often consoled me with thy compassion for my sorrows? Be comforted," she said to him; "Jesus sends me to thee to console thee; be comforted, rejoice, and come with me to paradise." And at these words the devout religious tranquilly expired, full of consolation and confidence.[20]

A prolific writer, tireless preacher, and relentless administrator and organizer, it is no wonder the Church has recognized Alphonsus's unusual zeal in spreading the Gospel and doing God's work. While Alphonsus vowed never to waste a minute of time, Fr. Santa believes that he may have been so driven, at least in part, by his scrupulosity. Saint Alphonsus was racked with a variety of physical and mental ailments throughout his life, from visual and respiratory problems to a possible nervous breakdown. Reportedly deaf, blind, and deformed by disease by the time of his death at age ninety, it is most pleasant to imagine this amazing, suffering saint when he receives a new glorified body after Christ comes again!

His feast day is August 1. St. Alphonsus Liguori, Most Zealous Doctor, Prince of Moral Theologians, pray for us, so that our battles with scruples may serve to cleanse our souls.

3
Love Conquers All — Including Scrupulosity

You who fear the Lord, trust in him,
and your reward will not fail;

You who fear the Lord, hope for good
things, for everlasting joy and mercy.

— Sirach 2:8–9

So faith, hope, love abide, these three;
but the greatest of these is love.

— 1 Corinthians 13:13

Every one of us should marvel at and never forget God's boundless generosity. We have seen how he endowed our natures with capacities to know truth and do good, perfected by intellectual and moral virtues. Hopefully we've begun to see how those wonderful natural virtues can help us overcome scrupulosity as well. But as the old, if grammatically infelicitous, saying goes, "You ain't seen nothin' yet!"

Scripture reveals three most special virtues that allow us to rise beyond the limits of our own nature through the grace of God. Enumerated by Yeshua ben Sirach in the Old Testament and by Saint Paul in the New, they are faith, hope, and love (or charity, from the Latin *caritas*). The Church tells us, "They inform and give life to all the moral virtues. They are infused by God into the souls of the faithful to make them capable of acting as his children and of meriting eternal life" (CCC 1813).

They are known as *supernatural virtues* because they are *super* (Latin for above or beyond) human nature alone, deriving from God himself. They are called *infused virtues*, because, as the *Catechism* notes, God infuses or pours them into our souls at baptism. They are known most formally as the *theological virtues*, deriving from the ancient Greek word *theos* for God. Thomas Aquinas, logical and organized as always, tells us three main reasons why we call faith, hope, and love theological virtues:

- first, because their object is God, inasmuch as they direct us aright to God
- second, because they are infused in us by God alone
- third, because these virtues are not made known to us, save by Divine Revelation, contained in Holy Writ (*ST*, I-II, q.62, a.1)

They are the most exciting and powerful virtues which God gives us out of his love so that we may embrace him in love.

They assist and raise our natural intellectual and moral virtues to a higher level here on earth, but they also open to us the doors of heaven so that one day we may enjoy eternity with him and the great communion of angels and saints.

The scrupulous may worry at times that through their thoughts, words, or deeds they have locked the gates of heaven against themselves, but God continually offers the heaven-opening keys of faith, hope, and charity for those who repent of real sins and desire to use these virtues to share his love. And as Scripture has told us, when our hearts are aflame with the love of God, the light of our love will also radiate out to our neighbors.

Let's dig in now to get to know better and appreciate more these three powerful virtues God placed within our hearts to help us better know and love him, our neighbors, and ourselves (and the better we know and love ourselves, the less paralyzed by scrupulosity we may be).

Faith: Trust in God Brings Temporal and Eternal Rewards

Faith, the first of the three theological virtues, lays the foundation for all the virtuous actions of a Christian. Reason (the "wing of reason" in JPII's metaphor), provides the foundation for natural, intellectual, and moral virtues. Faith does not contradict reason, but its wing lifts reason to higher realms of truth revealed by God, truths that unaided human reason alone cannot scale without God's assistance. The God-given virtue of faith then comes to inform and direct the natural cardinal virtues and all their fellow flyers by helping us grow in the knowledge and love of God, the source of all that is right and good. Saint Thomas declares, echoing Saint Augustine, that "there are no real virtues unless faith is presupposed" (*ST*, II-II, q.4, a.7). After all, we cannot hope for heaven, or love God with all that we are and our neighbors as ourselves, if we don't believe in God first!

Recall, if you will, our discussion of the natural virtue of religion, that assists us in just dealings with God. How does it relate to the supernatural virtue of faith that is also directed at God? Thomas tellingly provides a distinction that makes all the difference in the world, describing how the theological virtue of faith transcends the limits of the natural virtue of religion: "And yet the acts whereby God is worshipped do not reach out to God himself, as when we believe God we reach out to Him by believing; for which it was stated (see *ST*, II-II, q.81, a.1, 2, 4) that God is the object of faith, not only because we *believe in a God*, but because we *believe God*" (*ST*, II-II, q.81, a.5, emphasis added).

Note the subtlety of that last line. The virtue of faith goes further than the virtue of religion alone in providing an intimate, supernatural relationship with God. Recall that our opening verse from Sirach, in referring to faith, spoke of those who "trust in God," knowing he will gladly reward them as he has promised. A faith-driven "fear of God" says not only "God, I believe you exist, and I fear the punishment of hell," but "God, I *believe you*, and look forward to the reward of eternal joy with you!" Recalling again our brief excerpt from the *Catechism*, faith is the first of the virtues that makes us capable of acting as God's "children and of meriting eternal life."

Do you want to maximize the good and the joy your children experience? If you have no children, imagine if you did. Would you want them to experience eternal joy? After all, as Jesus once asked: "What man of you, if his son asks him for bread, will give him a stone? Or if he asks for a fish, will give him a serpent? If you then, who are evil, know how to give good gifts to your children, how much more will your Father who is in heaven give good things to those who ask him!" (Mt 7: 9–11). When we were baptized into the Catholic Faith, it was that loving Father who placed the virtue of faith in our souls. He wants us to trust in him so we'll thrive and grow, not suffer and fear.

Hope: Anticipating Boundless Mercy and Joy

In social science and medicine, a good deal of research shows that high levels of hope have been found to be associated with positive outcomes in all kinds of areas, including academic and athletic performance, physical and mental health, responsiveness to psychotherapy, and in helping inoculate children to feelings of loneliness. The human psychological disposition toward hope — a belief that one has what it takes to devise and carry out the plans to achieve one's goals — appears to confer substantial benefits in many areas, and very likely also in one's ability to conquer or better endure scrupulosity. Even on this earthly plane, the scrupulous have much to be hopeful for, since many people do indeed report cure or significant improvement through psychological and/or spiritual counseling and even, for some, through the long-acknowledged wound-healing powers that come with the passage of time. As many ailments such as back pain can resolve on their own with the passing of time, so too will some people with developmental scrupulosity come to find that they have "grown out if it."

Still, hope as a theological virtue bespeaks trust in a far higher power than our own capacities. With the God-given theological virtue of hope, our hopes for positive outcomes in the future extend to the most positive of all outcomes: eternal bliss with God in heaven! Further, through the theological virtue of hope, we need not depend merely upon on our feeble powers, but we can rely on the omnipotent power of God himself. We can say with Saint Paul, "I can do all things in him who strengthens me" (Phil 4:13). The theological virtue of hope presupposes our *desire* to spend eternity with God and our *confidence* that he will give us what we need to get there through the grace of the Holy Spirit. Those of us battling scrupulosity certainly have the desire component, but may be lacking in confidence. The more deeply we embrace the hope that God gives us, the more we will, as the saying goes: "Let go, and let God."

Charity: God's Love Can Help the Scrupulous Shine Our Lights before Men

That God is love itself could not have been revealed to us more clearly in words: "God is love" (1 Jn 4:8). That God wants us to share in his love could not have been revealed to us more clearly in actions: "For God so loved the world that he gave his only-begotten Son, that whoever believes in him should not perish but have eternal life. For God sent the Son into the world, not to condemn the world, but that the world might be saved through him" (Jn 3:16–17).

God offers his love to each and every one of us, so that our very bodies may be houses of his Holy Spirit (see 1 Cor 3:16–17; 6:19–20). Saint Paul made it clear that of the three theological virtues of faith, hope, and charity, it is charity that "never ends" (1 Cor 13:8) and is "the greatest of these."

How does only love endure forever? Through faith we believe in God and believe God, though we have not seen him. In heaven, blessed with the beatific vision, we will see and know God directly with no further need for faith. Through hope we look forward to bliss in heaven with God, trusting that he will supply us with what we need to get there. When we are already there, our hope for the future will be replaced by eternal reality. But as for love, it will not fade away, but will blaze more brightly than ever as we stand in the immediate presence of God himself who is love.

A deeper understanding and appreciation for the glorious, overflowing magnitude and eternal duration of the gift of God's love though the virtue of charity should lighten the burden of scrupulous souls who have mired themselves down with petty pebbles of scruples that God's love can cast aside. St. Thomas Aquinas has looked at the virtue of charity from a variety of angles from his lofty perspective as the Angelic Doctor. Let's examine just a few that might help us shrug off any sacks of scruples we've allowed to weigh us down.

First off, in his magnificent treatise on charity in the *Summa Theologica* (see II-II, q.23–46), Thomas addresses 143 articles (specific questions and answers) covering 116 pages in double-column print! Since we have somewhat tighter space restrictions here, I will simply begin with his very first insight and then move into another of his fascinating works on charity that may hold especially succinct and profound lessons for conquering scrupulosity.

Thomas begins his massive treatise on charity by explaining that it is a special kind of friendship, specifically, "the friendship of man for God" (*ST*, II-II, q.23, a.1). How do we know? Well, because the Bible tells us so! Jesus said, "No longer do I call you servants … but I have called you friends" (Jn 15:15). Saint Paul also told us, in the same letter in which he so elegantly explained the nature of love that "God is faithful, by whom you were called into the fellowship of his Son, Jesus Christ our Lord" (1 Cor 1:9). Jesus declared "Greater love has no man than this, that a man lay down his life for his friends. You are my friends if you do what I command you" (Jn 15:13–14). We know that he did indeed go on to lay down his life for us and that the greatest commands he gave us were commands to *love* God with all that we are and to love our neighbors as we love ourselves (see Mt 22:37–39; Mk 12:29–31; Lk 10:27).

Unfortunately, in a certain sense scrupulosity transforms Jesus' law of love into a law of fear. Fortunately, Saint Thomas has provided us with fascinating and hopefully helpful insights about the different classes of laws in a separate work on charity.[1]

Natural Law

God created the first humans, Adam and Eve, with a natural light to know right from wrong in terms of what we should or should not do. This *natural law* was present in human beings throughout all cultures. As Saint Paul wrote to the first century gentiles, who lacked the law of Moses:

> When Gentiles who have not the law do by nature what the law requires, they are a law to themselves, even though they do not have the law. They show that what the law requires is written on their hearts, while their conscience also bears witness and their conflicting thoughts accuse or perhaps excuse them on that day when, according to my gospel, God judges the secrets of men by Christ Jesus. (Romans 2:14–16)

This awareness of natural law lingers in us today. Thomas notes that "no one, for instance, is ignorant that he ought not to do to others what he is unwilling to have done to himself."[2] In our original state before we embraced sin, our actions readily followed the dictates of this natural light of understanding.

Law of Concupiscence

Through Satan's envy and Adam and Eve's prideful disobedience, however, sin and the law of concupiscence came into the world, so that, as Adam and Eve rebelled against God, our passions and lower natures gained the capacity to rebel against the natural light of our reason. Thomas cites Saint Paul, who stated so poignantly: "I see in my members another law at war with the law of my mind" (Rom 7:23).

Law of Scripture through Moses

Thankfully, however, God came to our aid to remedy this corruption by giving us the *law of Scripture* through Moses. Through this revelation, humanity came to hate sin, so as to avoid eternal punishment. Thomas notes that "the first reason anyone begins to avoid sin is the thought of the last judgment and hell."[3] This then is a law of fear. Indeed, not only is fear of the Lord the beginning of wisdom, but "the fear of the Lord driveth out sin" (Eccl 1:27, Douay-Rheims).

Law of Love through Jesus Christ

Jesus Christ brought us the fourth and the highest law of all when he gave us the *law of love.* Loving, filial fear casts out the imperfect servile fear of punishment, since, as Saint John told us, "perfect love casts out fear" (1 Jn 4:18). We will dive deep into the meanings and implications of "fear of the Lord" in our next chapter, when we examine its nature as a gift of the Holy Spirit. Christ's law of love is the highest of all laws, and should reign within our hearts. This is the law that matters the most and should guide and perfect the acts of our lives. Jesus' law of love is the lawbook the scrupulous should turn to. We'll find in it no long lists of petty transgressions and violations, but simple, positive commands of love, forgiveness, and mercy.

Thomas elaborates that Christ's law of love differs from and perfects Moses' law of fear in three essential ways:

1. Whereas the law of fear makes us slaves, the law of love makes us free, as Saint Paul says: "where the Spirit of the Lord is, there is freedom" (2 Cor 3:17).
2. The keepers of the first law were rewarded with temporal goods: "If you are willing and obedient, / you shall eat the good of the land" (Is 1:19). But the keepers of the new law are offered heavenly rewards; for example, in the words of Christ: "If you would enter life, keep the commandments" (Mt 19:17); and of St. John the Baptist: "Repent, for the kingdom of heaven is at hand" (Mt 3:2).
3. The yoke of the old law was heavy and burdensome,

as Saint Peter said to the Pharisees: "Why do you make trial of God by putting a yoke upon the neck of the disciples which neither our fathers nor we have been able to bear?" (Acts 15:10), but Christ said of his law, "My yoke is easy, and my burden is light" (Mt 11:30).

Let's make these three profound differences clear:

Key Differences in the Two Scriptural Laws

LAW OF MOSES	LAW OF JESUS
Fear	Love
Slaves	Freemen
Temporal rewards	Eternal rewards
Heavy	Light

The next time we encounter a scrupulous thought we should ask ourselves immediately which lawbook it comes from. Does it strike fear in our hearts? Does it bend our backs like a heavy load? If so, we are referencing a far too old edition, not the one that was transformed and perfected for our sakes by Jesus himself who loves us. He commanded us not to fear, but to love, not to bend in burden, but to carry light loads upright, not to shrink in the shadows, but to supercharge the natural light of our reason with the supernatural light of God's charity, and to become so busy figuring out how we can so shine that light of love among men that we have no time to waste worrying about past sins, let alone merely possible sins. Of course, it can be one thing to know such loving truths in our intellects and another thing to feel them in our hearts and will them in our actions. In the chapters ahead, we will continue to examine ways to help us make that leap from acknowledgment of God's love for us to acting it out in our lives, even if, at times, in spite of lingering doubts and fears.

Science of Scrupulosity — #3

The Causes of Scrupulosity

The exact cause of scrupulosity is not known. Like other forms of OCD, scrupulosity may be the result of several factors including genetic and environmental influences.

— International OCD Foundation[4]

Recalling that the virtue of science or knowledge seeks truths regarding causes and effects, we see that this human intellectual power has not yet reached its goal in mastering the exact cause of scrupulosity, but it has found several factors involved in nature and nurture that often go along with it. For example, some studies have shown correlations with genetically inherited factors — not that any particular "scrupulosity gene" has been found, but that scrupulosity and other forms of OCD have some tendencies to run more strongly in certain families. While the overall prevalence of OCD is about 2.3% for the population as a whole, various research studies show that when a person is diagnosed with OCD, the chance that a first degree relative has also been diagnosed varies from about 7% to 15%.[5] Unfortunately, we do not have precise data on the prevalence of religious scrupulosity in particular, which psychologists consider a subtype of OCD.

There are other biological findings that increase the likelihood that one will experience obsessions and compulsions, including neurological and psychiatric disorders like Parkinson's disease, Huntington's chorea, Tourette's disorder, certain epilepsies (seizure disorders), schizophrenia, and brain traumas and tumors. (Note well, this does *not* mean that most people battling scruples have one of these disorders!) Some studies suggest tendencies toward different patterns of activation in certain brain areas among some people with OCD, and other studies show that certain kinds of psychoactive drugs, such as SSRIs (selective serotonin reuptake inhibitors — such as well-known brand names of Prozac and Zoloft) help some people with obsessions and compulsions. That there can be biological connections with some forms of severe, persistent, obsessive-compulsive scrupulosity should come as no surprise, since God crafted us as integrated beings of body and soul.

Regarding *religious* scrupulosity in particular, our primary focus in this book, some people may suppose that religion itself is the cause of such scrupulosity, and yet even the secular research shows this is just not so! The International OCD Foundation notes that while "many notable religious leaders have struggled with this condition, including Saint Ignatius Loyola, Martin Luther, Saint Alphonsus Liguori, John Bunyan, and Saint Veronica Giullani … 'there is no evidence that the moral or religious character of scrupulosity sufferers is any different from that of other people.'"[6]

Some have also speculated that scrupulosity tends to be a Catholic thing. (Perhaps you've seen modern comedians who riff on their own experiences of "Catholic guilt" in their routines.) Again, the research shows this is not so. According to the International OCD Foundation: "Scrupulosity is an equal opportunity disorder. It can affect individuals from a variety of different faith traditions."[7]

Research has documented scrupulosity in people from a variety of religions — from Jews, to Muslims, to Hindus, to Protestants, to Catholics, though people of different beliefs may vary in the content of their scruples. For example, Turkish Muslim students scored higher than Canadian Christians on the PIOS Fear of God Scale (a subset of items of the PIOS Scale we featured in Science of Scrupulosity #1).[8] In the course of my research, I also came across a book written by a counselor aimed at treating scrupulosity among members of the Church of Jesus Christ of Latter Day Saints (Mormons).[9] I've seen speculation too, that perhaps for Catholics, scrupulosity was more common in the somewhat stricter pre-Vatican II era, and not so common now; but I know many priests who will attest that, unfortunately, scrupulosity is still alive and unwell in our time.

Back to religion in general as a possible "cause," we must recall that most religious people do *not* experience any severe or prolonged problems with scrupulosity. Second, we should note that some people who do not go to church and describe themselves as non-religious *do* experience religious scruples, fearing that they have offended God! Third, there is a related form of scrupulosity, found at times in both the religious and the non-religious, that can be called a *secular* or *moral* scrupulosity, centered on issues of right and wrong or potential harm to others without specific religious content.[10] That this kind of scrupulosity should exist should again be no surprise to Catholics. Let's recall these words of Saint Paul:

> When Gentiles who have not the law do by nature what the law requires, they are a law to themselves, even though they do not have the law. They show that what the law requires is written on their hearts, while their conscience also bears witness and their conflicting thoughts accuse or perhaps excuse them on that day when, according to my gospel, God judges the secrets of men by Christ Jesus. (Romans 2:14–16)

There is a "natural law" written in the hearts of every one of us, whether or not we realize it and recognize that it derives from God's "divine law." This human capacity of conscience, this innate capacity to discern right from wrong, is there in any one of us, and in certain circumstances can be misdirected into unneeded doubts and worries, into scrupulous thoughts and behaviors.

In addition to the common human nature we all share, as being made in God's image and likeness, with intellect and will, we are all unique individual persons as well, with unique learning experiences we encounter throughout life. Research also suggests that "obsessive fears and compulsive behaviors can be learned from watching family members or gradually learned over time."[11] Fortunately, means to conquer or cope with anxiety can also be learned, and modern psychotherapies have been developed that can help the scrupulous learn just what they need to know to overcome or lessen it. We'll start to dig into their lessons when we come to Science of Scrupulosity #4.

Saintly Lesson for Scrupulous Souls — #3

St. Thérèse of Lisieux (1873-1897)

As we'll consider more closely in chapter 6 on prayer, the saints in heaven sit willing to join their prayers to God with ours when we call upon them for their intercession. Now, certain saints really connect with each of us. Please pardon a personal story or two. If you can't tell already, I'm a St. Thomas Aquinas man, through and through — who wrote a bigger book than the over 1.5-million-word *Summa Theologica*!? His writings helped bring me back to Christ and the Church after twenty-five years as an atheist. And yet when I came back, another much less imposing saint who had a great impact on me was known for her "little way."

Saint Thérèse and I (and my family) have crossed paths many times over the years. When our local parish church was yet to be rebuilt, Kathy and I were married at the Church of the Little Flower (named after Saint Thérèse). A few years later, our sons would be baptized at her same church and would even graduate from her school.

Fast forward a couple of decades to just a few years ago, when I was invited to give a talk on the virtues at, of all places, Aquinas College (go Saint Thomas!) in Nashville, Tennessee. Well, the speaker before me, a professor, gave a fascinating talk on the harmful continuing influence of the atheistic nineteenth century philosopher Friedrich Nietzsche (whose writings I knew well as a youth). He mentioned in passing that it appears that Nietzsche happened to spend one night at the very same hotel in France at which Thérèse was staying with her parents. Perhaps the two even met! A fascinating thing to ponder, for their influences could hardly have been more different. Anyway, before I was introduced to speak, the emcee announced out loud (tongue in cheek) that the professor suggested that I, who happened to have had several books published recently, might write a book about the meeting of Nietzsche and Thérèse. I found it most amusing!

By the time it was my turn to speak, I announced to the audience (tongue in my cheek) that I'd decided to take up the task and had a potential title. Since it would be about how Nietzsche, author of *The Will to Power,* had met Thérèse, "the Little Flower," it would be called *The Will to Flower Power!* (It got some chuckles out of the young Dominican sisters in the front row, so it made my day!)

On a more serious note, little Thérèse, who lived her brief adult life within the walls of a convent, would become one of the best known and most beloved saints in modern times, and like the great Sts. Thomas Aquinas and Alphonsus Liguori, would even be declared a Doctor of the Church! She is dearly beloved for what she called her "little way" of loving and honoring God through the simple thoughts, deeds, acts, chores, prayers, and sufferings of our daily lives. In one short, sweet little prayer she would write:

> Throwing flowers means offering you, as first fruits,
> the least sighs, the deepest woes, my joys and my sorrows,
> my little sacrifices. These are my flowers.

Near the end of her life at age twenty-four, Thérèse suffered from the physical pains of tuberculosis, before they were relieved eternally in heaven on September 30, 1897. Earlier in her life she suffered from the mental and spiritual pains of scrupulosity, harboring dreadful fears that her sins offended God and rendered her unworthy of his love. Later, through growth in true knowledge of the Catholic Faith, continuing prayer, and spiritual direction, she was able to cherish the fact of God's mercy, as well as his justice. Realizing that he loved her (and each one of us) for the imperfect being she was, she developed her own "little way," to show God and neighbor her gratitude and love through all the normal, little things that can come to matter so much when done in the spirit of loving charity.

Thérèse can be a most powerful ally in the quest to cope with scrupulosity, both as an intercessor and as a source of great spiritual wisdom, including her insights on good will. In the words of a contemporary person who knows scrupulosity from firsthand experience:

> When you find yourself in an uncertain situation and don't know the best answer for moving ahead (scrupulous people most of the time), then you should say, "Lord, You know I want to do the right thing, even if it's not clear to me what that is, and instead of fearing for my soul or whether I'll be guilty of sin, I'm going to trust that You will take care of me and won't hold it against me if I make the wrong choice. I desire earnestly to please You, and that is enough." This is a mindset every scrupulous person needs to cultivate.[12]

Her feast day is October 1. Saint Thérèse, pray for us, that our pebbles of scrupulosity be transformed into little flowers of love.

4

The Holy Spirit Gives Gifts
to the Scrupulous

*The gifts are bestowed to assist the virtues, and
to remedy certain defects ... so that, seemingly,
they accomplish what the virtues cannot.*

— St. Thomas Aquinas, *ST*, I-II, q.68, a.8

*For God did not give us a spirit of timidity but
a spirit of power and love and self-control.*

— 2 Timothy 1:7

The virtues are perfections of our powers that operate by
bringing our thoughts, emotions, and actions under the
guidance of right reason, our highest, though fallible, natural

guide to the true and the good. We can employ them as powerful tools to help us combat scrupulosity as we come to better know them and practice them. Better yet, God has also made available to us seven *gifts* of the Holy Spirit that can guide our thoughts, feelings, and behaviors, not merely by human reason, but by the infallible inspiration of the Holy Spirit himself. The virtues have been described as oars on a boat that we use to row ourselves toward noble goals, while the gifts of the Holy Spirit are like massive sails that allow the wind of the Holy Spirit to carry us quickly toward godly goals on earth, and ultimately toward bliss with God in heaven. Here they are as they appear in the Bible: "There shall come forth a shoot from the stump of Jesse, / and a branch shall grow out of his roots. / And the Spirit of the LORD shall rest upon him, / the spirit of wisdom and understanding, / the spirit of counsel and might, / the spirit of knowledge and the fear of the LORD. / And his delight shall be in the fear of the LORD" (Is 11:1–3). Isaiah is prophesizing about the coming of Jesus Christ who would receive the Holy Spirit's gifts in their fullest measure, but the Church teaches that we *all* receive those same gifts at baptism and have them strengthened (made firm) at confirmation.

Per the *Catechism of the Catholic Church*: "The seven gifts of the Holy Spirit bestowed upon Christians are wisdom, understanding, counsel, fortitude, knowledge, piety, and fear of the Lord" (1845). If you wonder where piety came from, given the translation of Isaiah provided above, in Saint Jerome's Latin Vulgate Bible translation, from which the Catholic teaching arose, verse two ends with *pietatas*, "piety," and *timoris Domini*, "fear of the Lord," comes only at the end.

Medieval theologians noted long ago that there is a ranking of sorts among the gifts. They said Isaiah describes them from the highest (wisdom) down to the lowest (fear of the Lord) as they descend from the Holy Spirit upon man. And yet, if we arrange them in reverse order, they form a spiritual ladder through which we take the first step through fear of the Lord and eventually, having moved up the seven steps of the ladder, "there opens to us at the end of the ascent the entrance to the life of heaven."[1] We see this progression suggested several times in Scripture, where fear of the Lord is described as "the beginning of wisdom" (Ps 111 [110]:10; Prv 9:10; 15:33; Sir 1:14). Before we examine each gift, one-by-one, let's lay out this ladder and take a good look at it, since it may well help us climb farther away from scrupulosity as we move closer to heaven.

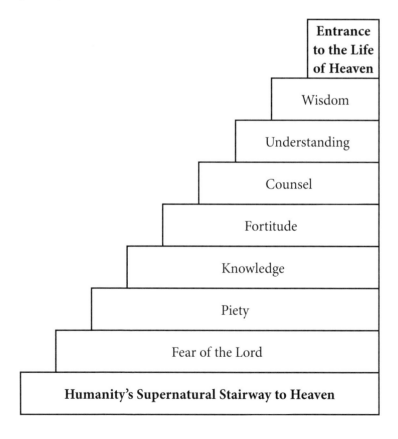

| Entrance to the Life of Heaven |
| Wisdom |
| Understanding |
| Counsel |
| Fortitude |
| Knowledge |
| Piety |
| Fear of the Lord |
| **Humanity's Supernatural Stairway to Heaven** |

A Spirit of Fear — but Not of Timidity!

Scripture tells us time and again that fear of the Lord is the beginning of wisdom. Our last chapter's opening verses from Sirach linked fear of the Lord to faith, hope, love, joy, unfailing rewards from God, and radiant hearts.[2] Further, the Holy Spirit stands ever ready to shower a proper fear of the Lord upon us freely as a gift. Sadly enough, for many of us battling with scrupulosity, an improper fear of the Lord brings needless suffering rather than joy. Our fear of the Lord should open our hearts and minds to all of God's other gifts, not paralyze us, through misplaced zeal, in morbid, self-focused scrutiny.

Twentieth-century spiritual writer Bernard J. Kelly, CSSp[3] observed that "scrupulous people are the victims of a false concept of law which they obey under the compulsion of fear."[4] (Does that "law of fear" ring any bells from our last chapter?) They perceive God as a tyrant and take no account of his mercy and kindness:

> They want to make their future salvation a certainty even now through their own efforts. He wishes them to be saved by His mercy and nothing else. They fret and agitate themselves, are always in action, for fear gives them no rest; He wishes them to surrender themselves fully into His hands, to leave their salvation to His Omnipotence.[5]

If, at this first step of our spiritual ladder, we should hope to avoid a "false concept" and "compulsion of fear" regarding the Holy Spirit's very gift of fear, who better than Saint Thomas to help us get our concepts straight?! As you might imagine, he has much to tell us about imperfect and perfect fear. Let's look at what he has to say:

Four Forms of Fear per St. Thomas Aquinas

Worldly fear	Fear of loss of earthly goods and pleasures
Servile fear	Fear of punishment
Initial fear	Fear blending servile and filial fear
Filial fear	Fear of committing a fault and offending God

Worldly fear is no gift of the Holy Spirit. It refers to our natural fears of losing the material goods or the sensual pleasures we desire and encountering privation, frustration, or physical pain instead. Neither is this kind of fear "the beginning of wisdom" (Ps 111:10). Jesus himself advised us, "Do not fear those who kill the body but cannot kill the soul" (Mt 10:28). By abandoning our worldly fears, we can focus our attention on a proper fear of the Lord: a fear infused with love, a fear lest we become less than what is fitting for creatures made in God's image.

What Saint Thomas — drawing on the writings of Saints Paul and John (see Rom 8:15; 1 Jn 4:17–18) — and the Church Fathers call **servile fear** is the lowest form of the Holy Spirit's gift of fear of the Lord. This is the fear of transgressing the laws of God out of a desire to avoid punishment. It is far from a perfect fear in that it is not inspired by the love of God for his own sake, but its object — the avoidance of God's displeasure and subsequent punishment — is good.

Initial fear derives from the Latin *initium,* "beginning." As the beginner starts to grow in a healthy fear of the Lord, servile fear and filial fear (a more perfect form of fear) might both be present. A man beginning to grow in charity, for example, might do the right thing both because he loves justice *and* because he fears being punished for misdeeds. As his love for justice grows with time, his servile fear of punishment will fade away. As we read in 1 Jn 4:18, "Fear has to do with punishment, and he who fears is not perfected in love." Further, "perfect love casts out fear."

As we grow in love, then, servile fear diminishes, and the increase of **filial fear** (from the Latin *filius/filia,* "son/daughter"), the last and most perfect form, leads to the perfect wisdom of charity. Filial, or *chaste* fear, conjoined with charity, is akin to the fear and deference that a son gives to his father or a wife to her husband out of affection and love. The object of this fear is the avoidance of committing a fault, a failing to live up to God's expectations for us, in much the same way we fear letting down a cherished member of our family. Note well, then, while scrupulosity warns us to fear God lest his wrath fall upon us, the Holy Spirit's gift of fear bids us to stand in wonder and awe before the Lord with the deepest sense of affection for him who gives us all that is good. Indeed, as Saint Paul reminds us, "In him we live and move and have our being" (Acts 17:28).

Seven hundred years after Saint Thomas wrote the *Summa Theologica,* when modern psychologists began building theories of the development of moral reasoning, they started with the avoidance of punishment at the bottom rung of the moral ladder, leading to concepts of perfect justice and love at its top. Indeed, the Holy Spirit calls us to strive continually to better ourselves, to develop our virtues with the aid of the gifts and make ourselves complete, for the greater glory of him who made us and showers us with his gifts. A healthy initial fear should inspire us to develop our God-given capacities for his honor and glory. Further, we should always recall what purely secular modern psychological theorists do not consider: that by the gifts of the Holy Spirit, starting with fear of the Lord, our moral acts are ultimately perfected by something beyond our psychological powers — namely, the stirrings of the Holy Spirit himself!

If our own fear of the Lord seems a little too high on the servile "fear" side, and a little too lacking on the filial "love" side, what can we do to grow in the kind of love that will cast aside the fear? While Saint Thomas tells us that the gifts can perfect the virtues, his great contemporary, the Franciscan Doctor of the Church Saint Bonaventure, points out that practice in virtue prepares us for use of those gifts (in a way that so appeals to the weightlifter in me): "Those who wish to have strong arms must give themselves to hard work. In a similar way, those who wish to have grace that strengthens them must give themselves to the practice of the virtues. The apostle states, 'By the grace of God I am what I am,' and then adds, 'I have labored more than all others.'"[6]

Note well too that Saint Paul's and Saint Bonaventure's labors were literally "labors of love." They did not merely decide to knuckle down and do hard things or to grin and bear difficult things through strenuous efforts of mere will power. Their labors were literally powered by their filial love of God. They never tired of contemplating the goodness of God and striving to show him gratitude in the everyday acts of their daily lives. Surely every parent can relate to the way that our love for our children empowers us to do difficult things, again and again, for many years on end. In fact, when we get toward the ends of our lives, we may look back in wonder on how we ever did it, until we remember how God's love strengthens us, his children!

Piety Loves God as a Loving Father

Each step up the ladder of the Holy Spirit's gifts builds upon the height we attain in the previous step. As initial fear blossoms toward filial fear, our predominant focus tends to change from

God as Judge of the living and the dead to the God who is love. As we step up the ladder to the gift of piety, our focus grows even clearer upon another astounding attribute of God. We saw that the virtue of piety treats of the honor we owe our earthly parents and our native land. The Holy Spirit's gift of piety enables us to honor and love God, not only as our Creator and Judge, but as our loving Father. According to Fr. Kelly: "Piety, then, in the sense of a gift of the Holy Ghost, is a power given us of submitting ourselves to the Holy Ghost breathing into our souls a spirit of childlike reverence for our Heavenly Father and of devotion to the furthering of His Interests."[7]

Jesus said, "Let the children come to me, and do not hinder them; for to such belongs the kingdom of heaven" (Mt 19:14). Have you ever had children? If not, do you remember being a child yourself? Think of all the mistakes we made as little children, all our misconceptions, and all the things we had yet to learn. Who among us did not go through the "terrible twos" for example: moody and temperamental, prone to screams, fits, and sometimes bites or hits, enraged upon hearing the word "No!" but quick perhaps to use it on others? Did our parents threaten to stop loving us and caring for us until we grew up and got our acts together? Of course not! A wise and loving parent loves us where we are and as we are, while slowly but surely guiding us, helping us grow and mature into the best, wisest, and most loving person we can become over time.

When we open our hearts to the Holy Spirit's gift of piety, we will more fully experience the reality of God Almighty as our all-loving Father, and the fact that all who share the Faith are members of his holy family. Do you have any close friends with children? If so, is there not a sense in which you love their children and wish the best for them, out of the love for your friend? It is through our love for God as Father that we also love Mary as our Mother, and all the great communion of saints in heaven, on earth, and in purgatory. We should never forget that we have a role to play in God's eternal family. When God the Son himself was asked how to pray, the first two words he uttered were, of course, "Our Father."

The scrupulous, who worry so much about their personal failings and possible sins, should heed well the words of Ven. Louis of Granada (1504–1588) about our spiritual family's willingness and ability to help us. He wrote specifically here about overcoming the sin of envy, but his lesson applies to our battle against any sin (or of our fears that we may have committed some sin):

> When you envy the virtue of another you are your own greatest enemy; for if you continue in a state of grace, united to your neighbor through charity, you have a share of all his good works, and the more he merits the richer you become. So far, therefore, from envying his virtue, you should find it a source of consolation. Alas! Because your neighbor is advancing, will you fall back? Ah! If you would love him in the virtues which you do not find in yourself, you would share in them through charity; the profit of his labors would also become yours.[8]

So wondrous is the treasury of merit of the communion of saints to which we are joined through the virtue of charity and gift of piety, that some scrupulous souls may someday find, to their surprise, that not only had they received profits from the labors of their brothers and sisters, but through their own persistent efforts to cope with scrupulosity, they may have accrued some merits that profited fellow sufferers.

From a developmental perspective, fear of the Lord is like a spiritual rebirth, and piety represents a new childhood, one that we must never completely outgrow, following the example of Christ, who faced temptations like you and me, but who always sought to please his Father and bring salvation to us, whom he made his brothers and sisters despite the ultimate sacrifice involved.

Knowledge Can Overpower Scrupulosity

Have you noticed yet that all of the gifts of the Holy Spirit (save fear of the Lord) have the same name as virtues we have already encountered in previous chapters? Well, Saint Thomas taught us that while there are great similarities between the virtues and the gifts of the same names, the difference that makes all the difference is that while natural virtues are guided by fallible human reason, the Holy Spirit's gifts make us amenable to the motions and guidance of the infallible Holy Spirit himself!

We encountered the *virtue* of knowledge (or science) as concerned with cause-and-effect relationships. Being guided by human reason, it operates on an inferential, sequential, step-by-step basis, since we acquire information piece by piece through our senses and then make sense of it all, so to speak, with our higher reasoning powers. Since the Holy Spirit knows all things at all times, when we are blessed by his gift of knowledge, it operates within us in an instant. As Thomas has made clear: "God's knowledge is not discursive, or argumentative, but absolute and simple, to which that knowledge is likened to a gift of the Holy Ghost, since it is a participated likeness thereof" (*ST*, II-II, q.9, a.1).

Strictly speaking, when contrasted with the highest gift of wisdom, the gift of knowledge progresses up the ladder toward wisdom by judging lower causes and effects that are of earthly and human matters, even though it addresses tenets of the Faith as well. While the *matters* of faith are themselves divine, the *virtue* of faith *that dwells within us* is limited, temporal, and exists within the mind of each one of us. The gift of knowledge then helps our minds grasp the ways that creatures mirror or reflect their Creator, and it gives us firm judgments about specific articles of faith that Christ's Church here on earth has declared to be true and worthy of belief.

As for that first function that lifts us up from the things of the world toward God, Scripture tells us that "from the greatness and beauty of created things / comes a corresponding perception of their Creator" (Wis 13:5), and, "Ever since the creation of the world his invisible nature, namely, his eternal power and deity, has been clearly perceived in the things that have been made" (Rom 1:20). The gift of knowledge can bring us powerful "Aha!" experiences, through which we realize God's majesty. Just think of anything that has ever awed or amazed you, from the mind-boggling magnificence of a galaxy brimming with billions of stars, to the cherubic beauty of a newborn baby's face. All of this comes from and reflects upon the glory of their Creator. It takes the great myriad of creation to reflect, in a dim way, what is totally present and one in God. The gift of knowledge helps make this clearer to us on earth, while we see through a "mirror dimly," before we see him face to face (see 1 Cor 13:12).

As for that second function pertaining to matters of faith, the great twentieth century Thomistic theologian, Fr. Reginald Garrigou-Lagrange, O.P., explained that "knowledge is a gift of the Holy Ghost which takes the form of right judgment in things that are to be believed, never confusing them with what ought not to be believed, once the Church has committed itself in deciding which is which."[9]

Thomas explains that the gift of knowledge gives us a sense of certitude within our minds about the truths of the Faith. However, faith also guides our actions, for it manifest as works, as Saint Paul wrote, faith works "by love" (Gal 5:6). In a certain sense then, the Holy Spirit's gift of knowledge and the certainty that it brings, can work directly to counter that sense of *uncertainty* that defines the "doubting disease" of scrupulosity, if we ask the Holy Spirit for an outpouring of knowledge and prepare our souls to soak it up. To the extent that we are receptive to this gift, charity will be free to bring our faith to life with good works directed towards others, perhaps helping damp down our doubts and fears at times, but enabling us better to act as we should even if some scruples remain in our souls. We may never feel absolutely certain about our own actions, but we can be certain that our faith is a true one and that God loves us so much that he has given us his Son, and his Holy Spirit.

Bearing in mind that exercising the virtues prepares us for receptivity to the gifts, every one of us should also exercise our minds and our reasoning capacities to grow in our knowledge of both earthly causes and effects, and in our knowledge of the essentials of the Faith. As for earthly causes and effects, as we examine current psychological methods of treating scrupulosity, we will come to learn how our own obsessive thoughts and compulsive rituals perpetuate a causal cycle that sustains scrupulosity. We'll also learn what we can do to break that cycle's chains. As for knowledge and certainty regarding the Faith, some scrupulous souls may be surprised to discover that they have committed themselves to far more than what the Church herself has determined is actually required of them.

Are you familiar, I wonder, with the "five precepts of the Church"? Well, sometimes confessors or spiritual directors direct people suffering from scrupulosity to back off on reception of certain sacraments (typically confession) or other holy activities for a time. When this happens, some scrupulous souls worry that God will condemn them for falling woefully short of what he expects of them. Well, behold the "five precepts" laid down by the Church "to guarantee to the faithful the very necessary minimum in the spirit of prayer and moral effort, in the growth in love of God and neighbor" (CCC 2041):

1. You shall attend Mass on Sunday and holy days of obligation and rest from servile labor.
2. You shall confess your sins at least once a year.
3. You shall receive the Sacrament of the Eucharist at least during the Easter season.
4. You shall observe days of fasting and abstinence established by the Church.
5. You shall help to provide for the needs of the Church according to your ability.

These represent the minimum for active Church membership and spiritual growth (summarized from CCC 2042–2043). This is not to say that more active participation cannot be better for some Catholics at some points in their lives, but it is to say that if you are suffering from scrupulosity and a priest has advised you to curtail your frequency of going to confession, for example, you can rest assured in the certainty of faith that the Church, as guided by the Holy Spirit's gift of knowledge, has declared God's truth, and this should leave you no room for doubt. Further, if any of the precepts themselves seem unclear to you, your spiritual director can clarify them and help ensure you live them out in your life.

The Fortitude that Never Fails

The mighty virtue of fortitude, guided by the best and strongest of human reason, will sometimes fail in its aim. The brave soldier whose fortitude allows him to overcome fear and face his enemy in battle may still be slain on the field. The brave soul whose fortitude allows her to enjoin battle against her own tendencies toward scrupulosity might never be completely victorious during her life on earth. Still, the mighty gift of fortitude, guided by the unconquerable Holy Spirit, will never fail in its ultimate aim, for even the martyr who, embracing this gift, dies for the glory of God, will overcome the most difficult of all obstacles, death itself, to attain the highest good of all: eternal bliss with God in heaven.

We read in the Book of Wisdom, "For the thoughts of mortal men are fearful, / and our counsels uncertain" (9:14, Douay-Rheims version). Indeed, there may be traces of fearful scrupulosity within us all, and yet, as Saint Bonaventure proclaimed, "Psalm 67[68]:35 professes: 'God is wonderful in his saints; the God of Israel himself will give power and fortitude to his people.' Therefore, fortitude is a gift of God."[10]

God still freely offers every one of us his gift of fortitude. It may or may not help us emerge victorious in our spiritual battles while here on earth, but it will certainly bring us ultimate victory in heaven, for "he who endures to the end will be saved" (Mt 24:13). We will peer deeper into the gift of fortitude in chapter 6 on the sacraments, particularly when we examine the Sacrament of Confirmation, which serves so well to strengthen fortitude. For now, let's ponder the prayer of our great scrupulous saint, Alphonsus Liguori, who bore his own cross during his life on earth that he might live to see the eternal day in which he would look upon the face of him who bore the true cross for us all: "Grant me the spirit of fortitude that I may bear my cross with Thee, and that I may overcome with courage all the obstacles that oppose my salvation."[11]

Counsel: As Prudent as the Holy Spirit

By embracing the gift of fear, we come to love God as our Creator. By embracing the gift of piety, we come to love God as a Father and our neighbors as our brothers and sisters in Christ. By embracing the gift of fortitude, we are strengthened to put such love into action. Now the Holy Spirit provides another gift, the gift of counsel, which guides and directs these other gifts, showing us just *how* to put them into action.

Warning against the uncertain counsels of men (see Wis 9:14),[12] the Holy Spirit then gives us access to counsel that is absolutely certain. Indeed, the Holy Spirit's gift of counsel has been called "the prudence of the Spirit."[13] Through this gift we can be guided by God's own limitless practical wisdom. Scripture tells us that "The Lord searches all hearts, and understands every plan and thought" (1 Chr 28:9). Think back to the virtue of prudence, if you will. God not only knows all our hearts, plans, and thoughts, he knows every outside circumstance, every past experience, every future contingency that could bear upon our actions. While the virtue of prudence is guided by right human reason, the Holy Spirit's gift of counsel is guided by the divine Logos, by Reason itself with a capital R!

Have you heard the old saying, "It takes one to know one"? Well, regarding those uncertain counsels of men, St. Alphonsus Liguori has offered what might sound as harsh counsel to the scrupulous regarding their scruples, until we recall that he included *himself* among them. Listen to a modern explication of the saint's great, unvarnished wisdom:

> According to Saint Alphonsus Liguori, the scrupulous must show blind obedience to the priest. He says that there must be no reasoning with them, because their imagination is a fool, and one does not reason with fools. That this obedience is obtained only with extreme difficulty, and very often not all, is known to all who have treated scruples. Since such a blind submission is extremely hard for the scrupulous, the priest must sustain and lead them vigorously.[14]

The Holy Spirit's counsel operates, if I might speak in the kind of language St. Thomas Aquinas is so fond of, in a twofold manner. First, the Holy Spirit can speak to our minds and hearts directly, but our minds and hearts must be ready. Scripture makes clear that sometimes the Spirit speaks to us in a still, small voice. While the world erupted around him in violent tumult, the prophet Elijah retired to a cave in Mount Horeb, the "mount of God." There he witnessed powerful winds that rent mountains, an earthquake, and then a great fire, "but the Lord was not in [them]," but after the fire came "a still small voice" (1 Kgs 19:12), and Elijah then went out to converse with the Lord, who instructed him where to go and what to do next.

We are all called to listen for the Spirit's "still small voice," though it is no easy thing to do if we are constantly bombarded by worldly distractions, by listening to the bad counselors out in the world, or to our own voices, for that matter, especially if they speak of scruples.

But the Holy Spirit also counsels us in a second way, a way of vital importance to those in the throes of scruples who would like to throw them away. On the level of natural virtue, Saint Thomas wrote of *eubolia* (good counsel) as an aid to the virtue of prudence. Thomas defines it as a natural "disposition to take good counsel" (*ST*, II-II, q.51, a.1) or advice from others about how to achieve virtuous goals. Saint Bonaventure warns that we must be careful from whom we seek counsel, reminding us of the counsel of Scripture: "Live in peace with many, but let one in a thousand be your counselor" (see Sir 6:6).[15] In the Holy Spirit's second way, he does not directly guide our minds to an answer, but guides us to seek counsel from the right person — the right one in a thousand — and, as noted before, to stick with that one and not shop around!

The scrupulous among us then, should gladly embrace this kind of counsel from the Holy Spirit, welcoming the chance to seek out good counsel from a confessor or spiritual director, to learn from him with docility, and to follow his counsel with obedience. Saint Alphonsus points out that the imagination of the scrupulous acts the fool, and the Book of Proverbs tells us that the fool who "rejects reproof goes astray" (10:17), "is right in his own eyes" (12:15), and repeats his folly "like a dog that returns to his vomit" (26:11). The wise person, to the contrary, "loves you when you reprove him; grows wiser from instruction" (see 9:8–9), "listens to advice" (12:15), and "lays up knowledge" (10:14).

May we all be open to the Holy Spirit's gift of counsel, whether he speaks to us directly or guides us to the earthly counselor he has in mind for us.

A Supernova of Understanding

We saw that through the natural virtue of understanding we are able to think at an abstract, conceptual level in terms of underlying principles. Indeed, Thomas tells us that "intelligence," his synonym for understanding, is related to the Latin words *intus,* for "inside," and *legere,* for "to read." Through our powers of understanding, humans alone among all beings on earth can read what is inside of things, grasping with our minds their fundamental natures or essences.

If you saw my white, fluffy, little fifteen-pound American Eskimo Lily next to my brother's golden-furred seventy-pound Retriever Randi, your intellect would read what's "inside" of both of them in an instant, and recognize that despite their differences, both them are "Ah, yes! *Canis lupus familiaris*!" (Okay, you would probably say dogs.) Of course, the conceptual powers that build upon our senses but take us so much further, can not only conceive of, name, and communicate with others about concrete critters like dogs, but also about abstract principles or spiritual realities, like "truth, justice, and the American way," or, higher yet, the seven gifts of the Holy Spirit.

Thomas calls these unique human powers of understanding

the "natural light" of our reason, which possesses the power to "penetrate to the heart of things." And yet he speaks of a much more powerful supernatural light as well: "Man needs a supernatural light in order to penetrate further still so as to know what it cannot know by its natural light: and this supernatural light which is bestowed on man is called the gift of understanding" (*ST*, II-II, q.8, a.1).

Compared to our human flashlights of understanding, the Holy Spirit's supernatural light of understanding is like a giant star's supernova! Still, while sojourning here on earth we can never completely understand the mysteries of God, but the gift of understanding can help us better grasp even this limitation.

In keeping with the celestial analogy, please join me on this journey of the imagination. Imagine you are in a pitch-dark room and in one corner lies a black hole. (We assume for our purposes that you are just outside the event horizon of the black hole and it has not sucked you in.) Surrounded by darkness, you have no clue that the hole is there. Now imagine you have been given a very powerful flashlight. Scanning the room, you now become aware of this fascinating, mysterious phenomenon. There it is! And yet, when you shine your light into the black hole, your eyes still lack the power to penetrate fully into its heart and show you just what it is at its core. The black hole remains mysterious and unfathomable, yet now you understand that it certainly exists, that it is right there with you, and that its awesome mystery exceeds your powers of full comprehension.

The gift of understanding is like a powerful supernatural light that illuminates our capacity to know God through faith and reason, to know that he is there even in our darkest hour (regardless of what our scruples might say), and to help us understand the very limits of our understanding while we live on earth. Of course, unlike our imagined black hole, God is not too dark to fathom. On the contrary, his light is too bright for the eyes that we have now, but one day, clad in our glorified bodies, he will illuminate our minds so that we will see his essence, to the extent it is possible for a glorified human being in heaven. So, while the essence of God himself exceeds the power of our light of understanding, the penetration which the Holy Spirit's gift of understanding provides for us can help us on our way toward that face-to-face meeting with God.

If we think about and embrace this marvelous gift, it should give us incentive and hope to rise above the petty concerns of our scruples, or at least to persevere in spite of them. The God who loves us is the God who made a universe brimming over with galaxies full of great stars and black holes. Who are we to doubt his power to haul us up to heaven if we are willing to grasp his outstretched hand? "For I, the LORD your God, / hold your right hand; / it is I who say to you, 'Fear not, / I will help you'" (Is 41:13).

Wisdom So Sweet You Can Taste It

The Holy Spirit invites us one and all to climb to the top of his spiritual ladder, where humble fear of the Lord has led us to the lofty gift of wisdom.

We saw that the natural virtue of wisdom judges the causes and effects deduced by science or knowledge and the principles arrived at through understanding. It is also the highest of the intellectual virtues because it judges of the highest and most fundamental of all causes. In philosophy this is called *metaphysics*, the study of things that underly and transcend even the laws of physics themselves — like why there are such laws in the first place. Wisdom even examines that ultimate cause of all effects and all subsequent causes, that Uncaused Cause which even the pagan Aristotle called God.

The Holy Spirit's gift of wisdom is the "wisdom from above,"

above even that of philosophy and metaphysics, about which Saint James speaks (see Jas 3:17). We should all strive to embrace this wisdom since "God loves nothing so much as the man who lives with wisdom. / For she is more beautiful than the sun, / and excels every constellation of the stars" (Wis 7:28–29). So just what is this great gift of wisdom, and how does it differ from the gift of knowledge? Let's ask a wise Thomist to find out.

We saw that while the gift of knowledge judges primarily of lower, earthly and human things, it can move us toward the consideration of higher things of God, but only indirectly, considering how earthly effects derive from higher causes. "The gift of wisdom," on the other hand, according to Fr. Reginald Garrigou-Lagrange, "proceeds in the opposite direction. It judges first of divine things, then of created things as insets of the divine."[16] In a fascinating insight into Scripture, Fr. Garrigou-Lagrange observes that the Gospel of Matthew may be seen to follow the path of the gift of knowledge in preaching Christ, starting with Christ's earthly genealogy and rising from the things of the earth to the things of heaven, while Saint John's Gospel starts right off with Christ as "the Word" in the first verse, "portraying in the higher light of wisdom that radiates from above, out through the lower streams of knowledge, with which Saint Matthew is more conversant."[17]

Saint Thomas tells us that while the gifts of knowledge and understanding flow from the theological virtue of faith, the gift of wisdom, the greatest of all gifts, flows from charity — the greatest of all the virtues (see 1 Cor 13:13). As with knowledge and understanding, the intellectual virtue of wisdom is built by our efforts and guided by human reason, but like God's other gifts, the gift of wisdom is infused in us by the Holy Spirit. It "comes down from above" (Jas 3:15).

Thomas declares that "wisdom which is a gift, has its cause in the will, which cause is charity, but it has its effect in the intellect, whose act is to judge aright" (*ST*, II-II, q.45, a.4). While the primary act of the intellect is to know the truth, the primary act of the will is to love the good. The gift of wisdom then empowers us, through the aid of the Holy Spirit, to grasp the highest truths of God of which our minds are capable, prompted by the ardent love of the highest good and source of all good — God! Joy is the emotion we experience when we attain what we love. The gift of wisdom helps us attain union with God in mind and in heart, and it brings with it great joy, joy that can overcome any suffering brought on by scruples.

And yet there is another very important (and delicious) quality of the gift of wisdom. Thomas tells us that the Latin word for wisdom, *sapientia,* is a contraction of *sapor,* "taste," "savor," or "flavor," and *scientia,* "science," which suggests that wisdom is a "sweet-tasting science" (*ST*, II-II, q.45, a.2). The psalmist calls us to "taste and see that the LORD is good!" (Ps 34[33]:8). We see God with the light of our intellects and savor him through the love in our hearts. Clearly then, the gift of wisdom has nothing to do with cold and tasteless abstractions. Neither does it fret or worry over the mere moral pebbles of quibbling scrupulosity. Rather, it is a gift that inflames our minds and hearts through a closer union with the goodness of God, a union that we savor and relish. We should want the gift of wisdom so badly that we can taste it!

Further, God has directed us to love him with all that we are and to love our neighbors as ourselves. The gift of wisdom, although primarily judging of the divine things of God, also has practical use in that it allows us to judge practical matters from a divine perspective, so that we may best serve our neighbors, sharing with them the fruits of charity and wisdom.

Unwrapping Your Own Gift Set
These marvelous gifts from the Holy Spirit were given to each

of us at baptism, strengthened at confirmation, and every time mortal sin has cut us off from their flow, restored to us instantly through reconciliation. They form God's holy ladder, through which we can rise above the scrupulous pebbles of earth and attain a glimpse (and a taste) of heaven while on earth. Let's do what we can to unwrap them, heeding Saint Bonaventure's advice to make ourselves amenable to the gifts of God's grace by rolling up our sleeves and working on the virtues, but also by simply allowing God to bestow those graces upon us, through prayer, reflection, and adoration. Indeed, a more modern saint, good Thérèse of Lisieux again, has compared God's graces not to a ladder, but to an *elevator*. There may be times when our own steps are not needed if we but allow God to lift us toward him by accepting his freely offered graces. And what better place to make use of God's elevator than within his own house through attendance at Mass and Eucharistic adoration?

In our next chapter, we will examine a very special means that Jesus Christ established to ensure that the highest of all graces will continue to give us spiritual strength throughout all our trials here on earth.

Science of Scrupulosity — #4

Wisdom 101: Exposure and Response Prevention to the Rescue

> *Victor Meyer (1966) published the first case of ERP for OCD. He reasoned that if individuals with OCD could be persuaded to remain in a fear situation and were prevented from carrying out the compulsion, then they would learn that the feared consequences of ritual nonperformance would not materialize (i.e., the conditioned fear stimulus is not associated with the unconditioned fear stimulus). This would result in modification of the obsessive-compulsive goal expectation, which in turn would lead to complete cessation of the compulsion.*
>
> — David A. Clark, Ph.D.[18]

We've seen that the virtue and gift of understanding perfects our powers to grasp the natures and underlying essences or principles of things. We've seen that the virtue and gift of science perfects our abilities to grasp causes and effects, how different things act upon one another producing specific results. Well, as Thomas noted before, the virtue and gift of wisdom judges both the principles of understanding and the causal relationships of science, and puts them into practice in our daily lives. In this Science of Scrupulosity essay, we will begin to examine what wisdom modern psychotherapists have gleaned regarding how to put our understanding of scrupulosity, and the scientific research behind it, into practices that can help cure it.

From our quotation above, we see that the psychotherapeutic method now called Exposure and Response Prevention (ERP) for obsessive-compulsive disorders got its official start back in 1966, but even now it is considered the gold standard for psychological treatment of the various forms of OCD, including scrupulosity. Numerous studies over the decades have shown symptom improvement from ERP in 60–85% of the patients treated with it, and that should be very encouraging.[19] Most psychological treatments of OCD today include ERP, either on its own or as part of a more comprehensive treatment plan. (Other approaches will be addressed in the remaining Science of Scrupulosity essays.) While I can direct you, if interested, to sources with more detailed treatment of the ERP procedure itself,[20] we'll take a few minutes here to examine both its rationale and its use in dealing with scrupulosity.

Exposure and Response Prevention treatment is based on the "anxiety-reduction hypothesis." *Obsessions,* that is, unwanted, intrusive scrupulous thoughts or images — whether of blasphemy, damnation, sexual impurity, violent impulses, whatever the case may be — produce distress and anxiety. *Compulsions,* that is, ritualistic external acts or mental behaviors — whether of frequent confession, seeking reassurance from others, avoiding communion, repeating mental prayers, making "deals" with God, whatever the case may be — are performed in an attempt to reduce the anxiety produced by the obsessive thoughts or images. Oftentimes, however, the compulsions do not reduce the anxiety for long, or may even increase it if the scrupulous fear they have not performed their compulsive rituals correctly. This typically turns into a vicious cycle of recurring distressing obsessions and compulsions.

ERP seeks to *desensitize* a person to their obsessive thoughts or images by allowing them to experience them, and the anxiety they produce, while their response (their compulsions) is prevented from occurring — usually at first in an office with their therapist. The person typically finds through repeated exercise of this procedure, systematically arranged to correspond to his own particular scruples, that he can cope with the anxiety without compulsive responses, and that anxiety itself, over time, becomes quite endurable and may fade completely away.

Working with a therapist, the client prepares a list of maybe ten or a dozen various situations or behaviors that produce obsessions and compulsions for him, and ranks them from least to most severe. This is most easily seen in cases of non-religious obsessions and compulsions: for example, those regarding cleanliness or fear of contamination from germs. Dr. Davidson, in *Daring to Challenge OCD*, provides a simple example of a woman with contamination obsessions who listed ten such situations, ranked by the patient from a personal distress score of 15 for touching forms sitting on the therapist's desk to 100 for using the restroom in the doctor's office where other patients might be ill. Right in the middle were behaviors like using the door keypad in the therapist's office or sitting on a public park bench. In the basic procedure, the patient starts by performing the least stressful behavior (touching the papers on the therapist's desk), but without performing her typical compulsive response of immediately pulling out and using her hand sanitizer. This might be repeated several times with different fingers, and perhaps eventually with both hands.

Even the very act of producing one's list of stressors can produce anxiety in many patients, since it forces them to think about the things that make them anxious. Still, merely this initial mental exposure can be beneficial in training them to face or lean into their anxiety. Over time, in a series of sessions, the patient works with the therapist to master increasingly anxiety-producing situations without the need to counter with compulsions.

The client is often surprised to find that nothing bad happens when they do not counter their obsession with a compulsion, that they can cope with the anxiety, and that the anxiety fades with time. In essence, they learn, and experience, a new, effective way of dealing with intrusive thoughts.

If we might draw a connection back to St. John Climacus's six stages whereby a tempting thought or image may or may not turn into a sinful passion, the patient learns to nip things in the bud at the first stages, recognizing that a "provocation" (temptation or intrusive thought or image) has occurred, but at the second "coupling" phase, in which one converses with oneself about it, the whole conversation is changed. One forgoes the struggles and potential defeat of the subsequent stages by calmly telling oneself that this is merely an intrusive thought or a scruple and it will soon pass if one refuses to struggle or pay it heed.

The therapist may also assign the client some related homework to do between sessions. Sometimes the anxiety-reducing exercises may be performed simply by *imagining* the situations, rather than actually experiencing them. This too can help desensitize the patient and reduce anxiety and the need for compulsive responses.

There are special concerns, however, for employing ERP for religious scrupulosity. Some therapists who are unfamiliar with a person's faith (or even a small minority of therapists, whom we might say ironically could be called "unscrupulous" themselves), might encourage a patient to construct an exposure hierarchy of scruples-inducing situations that encourage actual sinful behaviors. Summers and Sinnott-Armstrong give examples of therapists who might, for example, encourage a client with fears of blasphemy to actually blaspheme, or encourage a client who fears blurting out racial slurs in public to blurt them out during a therapy session. Such behaviors in session could be sinful on their own, and could also become the source of new scruples for the patient for having done them. Indeed, it is estimated that about 20–30% of patients with all forms of OCD simply refuse to do ERP.[21]

For this reason, if religious scruples are to be treated with ERP by a psychotherapist, it is ideal if the psychotherapist is well-versed in the client's particular religious faith. If the patient is Catholic, the therapist could also consult the patient's priest. The patient might consider giving his or her priest permission to discuss his or her situation with the therapist.[22]

In any event, the structured use of ERP has a very good track record in helping people whose scruples and other obsessions and compulsions are so severe and distressing that formal therapy is in order. It appears to be a sturdy wing of reason that can help many people of faith fly above and beyond scrupulosity.

Saintly Lesson on Scrupulosity — #4

St. Katherine Drexel (1858–1955)

Another saint who struggled with scruples has crossed the path of my family and me, as we are currently members of a St. Katherine Drexel Parish! I cannot help but see some parallels in the life of this saint with the life of St. Thomas Aquinas. Both were born into families of considerable wealth and influence: Thomas to a noble family near Aquino, Italy, and Katherine to the richest family in Philadelphia, Pennsylvania. Both forsook the pursuit of wealth and power and became members of religious orders: Thomas joining the relatively new Order of Preachers (Dominicans), vow of poverty and all, and Katherine joining the Sisters of Mercy and eventually forming her own order, the Sisters of the Blessed Sacrament for Indians and Colored People, that catered to educating the poor and needy Native American and African-American populations. Katherine's natural inclinations drew her toward the contemplative life, with a special mystical devotion to the Eucharist, but her spiritual directors and advisers directed her toward the active life. Thomas, embracing the value of both as well, would famously write that "for even as it is better to enlighten than merely to shine, so is it better to give to others the fruits of one's contemplation than merely to contemplate" (*ST*, II-II, q.188, a.6).

Katherine and the sisters of her order constantly shared their monetary resources[23] and their spiritual fruits with the people most direly in need of physical and spiritual nourishment.

The magnitude of Saint Katherine's corporal and spiritual works of mercy throughout her ninety-seven years on earth were truly remarkable, and arose despite difficulties she experienced with scrupulosity in her youth. Her spiritual director, Fr. James O'Connor of Philadelphia who later became Bishop O'Connor of Omaha, Nebraska, counseled her on her scruples and warned her against excesses in activities like fasting.

She obeyed the good bishop, conquered her scruples, and helped conquer poverty and ignorance of Christ among the Native American and African-American peoples of the United States of America. Her feast day is March 3.

St. Katherine Drexel, pray for us that we might overcome a scrupulous concern with our own faults, that we might better share the fruits of our contemplation with our brothers and sisters who need them the most.

5

Scrupulosity and the Healing Power of the Sacraments

Properly speaking a sacrament, as considered by us now, is defined as being the "sign of a holy thing so far as it makes men holy."

— St. Thomas Aquinas, *ST*, III, q.60, a.2

Reception of Communion is a defining moment for people with scrupulosity. If the confession of sins is an experience of anxiety, it's the reception of Communion and its rituals, rules, and conditions that fuel the scrupulous conscience.

— Fr. Thomas M. Santa, CSsR[1]

It is an unfortunate fact that the very gifts Jesus gave to his Church to help us grow in holiness often become twisted by scrupulosity into sources of fear and foreboding.[2] First off, if you are suffering with scrupulosity, you should be well aware that you are not alone when it comes to worrying about the sacraments — indeed, precisely as Fr. Santa has told us, foremost among them are the Sacraments of Reconciliation (confession or penance) and the Eucharist (communion). Here we will try to convert such feelings of fear into hope and heartfelt gratitude to God for inviting us to share in his intimate life, and freely offering us the precise means we need to do so. So, guided by Saint Thomas and other great lights of the Church, let's move through the sacraments as a whole, and then one-by-one, so that we might see them more clearly, not as signs of worry and dread, but as vehicles toward to holiness, happiness, and peace.

So, Just What Is a Sacrament?

Thomas told us that a sacrament is a "sign of a holy thing so far as it makes men holy" (*ST*, III, q.60, a.2).[3] Signs are sensible, familiar things that point to things other than the signs themselves. It is part of human nature to acquire knowledge of higher things through the information that comes in from the senses. In the sacraments of the Church, visible, material things such as water, oil, bread, and wine point to the invisible, but real and powerful graces poured into us by God. Those graces serve to perfect our holiness in a variety of ways particular to each of the Church's sacraments.

Sacraments are also means of worshiping God. In addition to sensible, material signs, sacraments employ words as signs of our sanctification. This is most appropriate for several reasons:

- First, the sacraments use words that speak of the cause of our sanctification — which is the Word

Incarnate. In this way, the sacraments bear resemblance to Christ, who initiated them. Sacraments join words to material signs, as in the Incarnation wherein the Word was joined to sensible flesh.

- Second, as we who are sanctified by the sacraments are composed of soul and body, the sacraments touch the body through the material elements and the soul through faith in the words.

- Third, words are the primary means by which we express ideas with greatest clarity. For example, "when we say, 'I baptize thee,' it is clear we use water in baptism in order to signify a spiritual cleansing" (*ST*, III, q.60, a.6) rather than merely to cleanse or cool the body.

Why Do We Need Sacraments when Christ Died for Our Salvation?

Some argued in Thomas's day and before (and some still do!) that we do not need the Church's sacraments. After all, Christ told Saint Paul, "My grace is sufficient for you" (2 Cor 12:9). Why would we need sacraments when Christ's grace suffices? When a cause is sufficient to produce an effect, nothing else is needed. We are told in Romans 5:10 that we were reconciled to God by Christ's death and saved by his life. Christ died and rose to achieve our salvation. Why on earth would we need sacraments?

Thomas answers that, for salvation, humanity must be united in the one true religion. Augustine notes that one cannot keep people within one religious denomination unless they are united by common, visible signs or sacraments. Sacraments are needed for salvation because our God-given human nature requires that our minds be led to spiritual things by bodily and material things. We form concepts from precepts, built upon bodily sensations. This is, in part, because we are diseased in sin by inappropriate love for bodily things and pleasures, and it is appropriate that God provides a spiritual medicine that also works through the senses. The sacraments provide the right bodily exercises — ones that draw us away from improper worship and harmful, sinful actions. It is of the greatest importance to note, in response to objections, that Christ's passion is indeed the sufficient cause of our salvation, but the sacraments obtain their power through his passion. "Christ's Passion is, so to say, applied to men through the sacraments" (*ST*, III, q.61, a.1).[4]

What Effects Can Sacraments Have on Us?

First, the sacraments provide us with God's grace, and grace is an awesome thing! Thomas writes, "Grace is nothing else than a participated likeness of the Divine Nature, according to 2 Peter 1:4: 'He hath given us most great and precious promises; that we may be [Vulgate — 'you may be made'] partakers of the Divine Nature'" (*ST*, III, q.62, a.1). Sacraments do not merely point to higher, spiritual things. They are "both causes and signs," which is to say, "They effect what they signify" (*ST*, III, q.62, a.1). Sacraments, we might say, don't just talk about it, they get the job done. As the sun's powerful rays bring warmth and health to our bodies, God's sacraments radiate his all-powerful grace to heal and strengthen our souls. And, as we soon will see, the "jobs" the sacraments do serve to perfect us spiritually in a great variety of ways. They help perfect all kinds of virtues, are remedies for all kinds of sins, and indeed, as well, for worries and doubts about merely possible sins.

Sacraments, Virtues, and Spiritual Growth

As Thomas wrote so eloquently, "The Church is said to be built up with the sacraments 'which flowed from the side of Christ while hanging on the Cross'" (*ST*, III, q.64, a.2). Building upon

God's gift of seven sacraments, Church Fathers have noted their special relationship to the seven virtues (our familiar four cardinal and three theological virtues), as well as to seven bodily and social perfections that develop throughout human life. Let's lay them all out on the table, so to speak, before we taste of each sacrament one-by-one.

A Sacred Sevens Side-by-Side

SACRAMENT	VIRTUE	BODILY AND SOCIAL HUMAN PERFECTIONS
Baptism	Faith	Birth
Confirmation	Fortitude	Growth
Eucharist	Charity	Nourishment
Reconciliation	Justice	Healing sickness
Anointing of the Sick	Hope	Restoration of Health and Vigor
Holy Orders	Prudence	Governance and Public Acts
Matrimony	Temperance	Propagation of the Species

Baptism: Our Rebirth in the Faith

"Our Lord said (Jn 3:5); 'Unless a man be born again of water and the Holy Ghost, he cannot enter into the kingdom of God'" (*ST*, III, q.60, a.5). Through baptism, we are spiritually reborn into the family of the King of all kings, with the Blessed Mother as our mother, and the great communion of saints in heaven, on earth, and in purgatory as our brothers and sisters. Baptism has been called "the door of the sacraments," because "it confers on man the power to receive other sacraments of the Church" (*ST*, III, q.63, a.6). Baptism washes away original sin and makes us members of the Body of Christ, producing in us an indelible mark or character through the power of Christ's passion and resurrection. The visible sign of water represents the cleansing of sin, and also our rebirth in Christ.

The Sacrament of Baptism does not appear to be a common subject of scrupulous thoughts, thanks be to God![5] Nor should it be. The ritual is pretty straightforward. While immersing or sprinkling the recipient with water, the Church heeds Christ's explicit instructions under this form: "I baptize thee in the name of the Father, and of the Son, and of the Holy Ghost; whereas the Greeks use the following form: The servant of God, N… is baptized in the name of the Father, etc." (*ST*, III, q.60, a.8).[6] Ideally, a baptism is performed by a priest in the context of an entire liturgical rite, but this is not necessary for a valid baptism.

Because of the indelible character of a valid baptism — using water and done in the name of the Father, the Son, and the Holy Spirit — Thomas reported that the Church would consider valid such baptisms performed by people who were not priests: by laymen, by heretics, indeed, even by "pagans," or non-Christians, should need arise in case of dire emergencies. He even provides an extreme example of two pagans facing death who desired to be baptized — wherein one could baptize the other, who in turn would baptize him (*ST*, III, q.67, a.6). If you have been baptized with water at some time in your life, in the name of the Father, the Son, and the Holy Spirit, even if outside the Catholic Church, you need not spend time worrying that you were not baptized.[7] Indeed, even for those who never get to receive the water and words of the Sacrament of Baptism, the Church duly recognizes the "baptism of desire." A person desiring baptism who dies before receiving it "can obtain salvation without being actually baptized, on account of his desire for Baptism, which desire is the outcome of faith that worketh by charity, whereby God, Whose power is not tied to visible sacraments, sanctifies man inwardly" (*ST*, III, q.68. a.2).[8]

Clearly then, baptism should be no subject of scrupulous thoughts, but an aid in curing them, since it opens up the door to faith, provides spiritual rebirth, makes us members of God's family, and allows the infusion into our hearts of faith, hope, charity, and all the Holy Spirit's gifts that flow from them to our aid.

Confirmation Can Give Us the Fortitude to Grow Beyond Scrupulosity

Saint Thomas tells us that while Christ did not confirm anyone himself (neither did he baptize):

> We must say that Christ instituted this sacrament not by bestowing, but by promising it, according to John 16:7: "If I go not, the Paraclete will not come to you, but if I go, I will send Him to you." And this was because in this sacrament the fulness of the Holy Ghost is bestowed, which was not to be given before Christ's Resurrection and Ascension; according to John 7:39: "As yet the Spirit was not given, because Jesus was not yet glorified." (*ST*, III, q.72, a.1)

We have seen that the grace of baptism produces a spiritual birth. Spiritual growth can be seen to parallel bodily growth in man. The child moves toward perfection of his powers as he approaches adulthood with the ability to act as an adult — hence the apostle says, "When I became a man, I gave up childish ways" (1 Cor 13:11). Through the grace of confirmation, we are strengthened in the maturity of our faith by a special outpouring of the Holy Spirit, which includes, as we saw in our last chapter, the Holy Spirit's gift of fortitude. Indeed, in the Sacrament of Confirmation, the bishop prays that God send his Holy Spirit upon the confirmation candidates, invoking all seven gifts by name.

And why does a bishop administer this sacrament? "Though he who is baptized is made a member of the Church, nevertheless he is not yet enrolled as a Christian soldier. And therefore he is brought to the bishop, as to the commander of the army" (*ST*, III, q.72, a.10). Every man and woman is called to be a Christian soldier, engaged in spiritual warfare, but armed with the gifts of God's supernatural weapons. Some Christian soldiers will find they must battle scrupulosity too, but they must never forget that God has confirmed them — literally made them "firm" and strong — to overcome, or at least endure, their scruples without surrender.

The Eucharist Nourishes Us with God's Love (and with God Himself)

Sadly, Christ's greatest gift to us while here on earth, his own Body, Blood, Soul, and Divinity in the Holy Eucharist, is often a great source of suffering among scrupulous souls. In his masterful *Understanding Scrupulosity,* Fr. Santa devotes an entire chapter to "Questions About Holy Communion." We will look at common scruples regarding Communion, and what to do about them, and then we'll take a deeper look at this greatest of sacraments itself.

Perhaps the most common source of scrupulosity regarding receiving Communion comes from a misunderstanding of Saint Paul's words: "Whoever, therefore, eats the bread or drinks the cup of the Lord in an unworthy manner will be guilty of profaning the body and blood of the Lord. Let a man examine himself, and so eat of the bread and drink of the cup. For anyone who eats and drinks without discerning the body eats and drinks judgment upon himself" (1 Cor 11:27–29).

The scrupulous person may feel unworthy to receive Communion, fearing he or she may have committed (or improperly confessed, which we'll address in our next section) all sorts of sins or possible sins, some of which relate directly to Communion itself. Not to add fodder to scrupulous tendencies, but to show the scrupulous that they are not alone, worries expressed to priests include such minor concerns about foregoing Communion because one had to take medicine, brushed their teeth, used mouthwash, or even merely wore lipstick within an hour of Communion. Such trivial concerns should never keep us from receiving Our Lord.

Others worry about the particles of the Host. What if they have taken Communion in the hand and some particles have dropped to the floor? In the words of Fr. L. Miller, CSsR, "The Lord knows how to take care of himself if he is actually on the floor. And anyway, the white particles (if seen on the floor) may be lint or paper or almost anything. Don't worry if you see the floor so covered. Do nothing about it."[9] St. Philip Neri (1515–1595) is sometimes cited as the source of this insightful quotation on this same topic of worry over crumbs from the host: "Leave it to the angels. They need something to do."[10]

A far more serious matter is actual sins that could render us unworthy to receive Communion — before confession and repentance. Indeed, of special concern in our time is debate over prominent Catholic politicians who publicly promote grave evils contrary to Church teaching and natural law, like abortion. Let's listen to St. Thomas Aquinas on this matter.

In the third part of his *Summa Theologica,* in the sixth article of question 80, Thomas addresses head on "Whether the Priest Ought to Deny the Body of Christ to the Sinner Seeking It." Citing Saint Augustine on the fact that all of us are sinners, the answer to that question in general (and for the scrupulous!) is, "No!" However, "a distinction must be made among sinners; some are secret; others are notorious, either from evidence of the fact, as public usurers or public robbers, or from being denounced as evil men by some ecclesiastical or civil tribunal. Therefore, Holy Communion ought not to be given to open sinners when they ask for it."

Note the difference that makes all the difference between "secret" sinners, as are most of us, and "public" sinners who openly scandalize others and may lead them to sin. Indeed, for the scrupulous some of their supposed sins may be "secret" even unto themselves, since they worry that they simply "might have" sinned. The spiritual food such scrupulous souls are most in need of is the Eucharist itself, since it nourishes us with Christ's loving gift of self.

Many great saints and Doctors of the Church, like Thomas Aquinas and his contemporary Saint Bonaventure, explained that when Christ taught us to pray the Our Father, the petition "give us this day our daily bread," foretold the day when that nourishing bread would include his own sacramental presence in the Eucharist. Indeed, our great and scrupulous doctor, St. Alphonsus Liguori, says that "people with scrupulosity should receive Communion unless they're absolutely certain they have sinned mortally."[11] This statement bears repeating. The man declared by the Church as the "Prince of Moral Theologians" says that *"people with scrupulosity should receive Communion unless they're absolutely certain they have sinned mortally."* And if I might add one last emphasis, note well the words "absolutely certain"! Modern day Redemptorist priests note that for our simple, daily, venial offenses, a sincere Act of Contrition, as is said during Mass in the Penitential Rite, opens us to God's forgiveness so that we may accept his invitation to receive him in the Eucharist. The Eucharist is not a poison, but the greatest of spiritual food. We should express our gratitude to God by regularly receiving the Eucharist. Though we are not worthy without God's grace, he willingly comes under the roofs of our mouths so that our souls may be healed.[12]

Let's end our consideration of the Eucharist by pondering a couple of verses from beautifully sublime prayers from the "Eucharistic Doctor" himself, St. Thomas Aquinas.[13] The first verse you have probably heard sung by great singers such as Luciano Pavarotti or Andrea Bocelli:

> The Bread of the Angels now is Bread of man.
> Heavenly Bread fulfills what prophecies foreshadow.
> O wondrous thing! God is consumed
> By the poor, the humble, and the low.[14]

Not sounding familiar? Well, you've heard the verse sung like this:

> Panis angelicus fit panis hominum.
> Dat panis caelicus figuris terminum.
> O res mirabilis! Manducat Dominum
> Pauper, servus et humilis.

Note the exquisite rhyming and flowing rhythm of the popular *Panis Angelicus* in Thomas's original Latin (and listen to it on the internet the next time you get a chance!).

Here is an appetizing tidbit, where Thomas describes his

hunger for the Eucharist and for seeing Christ face to face one day in heaven:

> Devoutly I adore you, hidden deity,
> Under these appearances concealed,
> To you my heart surrenders self
> For seeing you, all else must yield ...
> Jesus, whom I see enveiled,
> What I desire, when will it be?[15]

May we burn with such desire for the Eucharist here on earth and for Christ himself in heaven that no scruple will stand in our way. Let's ponder too that Thomas tells us one of our greatest joys in heaven will to be gaze upon Jesus Christ in the flesh!

Reconciliation: A Sacrament Not of Fear, but of Justice and Healing

Here we come to a second sacrament of special concern to the scrupulous. Most interestingly, the *Catechism* tells us this multi-faceted sacrament is actually called by five names (1423–1424, abridged below). This sacrament is called:

1. the *sacrament of conversion* because it makes sacramentally present Jesus' call to conversion, the first step in returning to the Father from whom one has strayed by sin.
2. the *sacrament of Penance,* since it consecrates the Christian sinner's personal and ecclesial steps of conversion, penance, and satisfaction.
3. the *sacrament of confession,* since the disclosure or confession of sins to a priest is an essential element of this sacrament.
4. the *sacrament of forgiveness,* since by the priest's sac-

ramental absolution God grants the penitent "pardon and peace."

5. the *sacrament of reconciliation*, because it imparts to the sinner the love of God who reconciles: "Be reconciled to God." He who lives by God's merciful love is ready to respond to the Lord's call: "Go; first be reconciled to your brother."

It seems that scrupulosity can cause souls to focus too much on that third element of the name of *confession,* so tied into the revealing of one's sins to a priest, that they may overlook the other elements to their peril of needless suffering. In Fr. Wade Menezes, CPM's excellent internet article, "10 Commandments for Those Who Struggle with Scrupulosity," a full *nine* of the ten commandments for the scrupulous explicitly address this sacrament (while the one that does not mention confession distinguishes between temptation and sin, the stuff of our chapter 1).

Let's see what good Father Wade advises:[16]

TEN COMMANDMENTS FOR THOSE WHO STRUGGLE WITH SCRUPULOSITY

1. Do not repeat prayers, no matter how badly they may have been prayed, even if the prayers were given to you as a penance during the Sacrament of Reconciliation (confession).
2. Do not repeat the confession of sins that have already been confessed and which have never been recommitted.
3. If you doubt the earnestness of your sorrow in confession, consider the sorrow as having been adequate.
4. If you are doubtful as to whether a past action you committed was sinful, mention it simply to your con-

fessor (i.e., without a lot of great and/or graphic detail).

5. If you are worrying that maybe you never confessed a certain sin from your past, consider it confessed. If you know for a fact that you have never confessed that sin, then confess it simply (i.e., without a lot of great and/or graphic detail). The Holy Spirit does not torment us with doubt and/or guilt; rather, he always brings peace as he awakens our conscience to our sins. (see 2 Cor 7:10–11: "Indeed, sorrow for God's sake produces a repentance without regrets, leading to salvation, whereas worldly sorrow brings death. Just look at the fruit of this sorrow, which stems from God. What a measure of holy zeal it has brought you!")

6. Examine your conscience for no longer than three minutes each day, and for no longer than about ten minutes before you go to confession.

7. If you have prayed at the time of temptation (i.e., precisely to help dispel the temptation), you can be sure you did not commit a mortal sin.

8. If you have a history of scrupulosity, and you have made a general confession at some time in your past, do not make another general confession. Once a month is a good norm/interval for the frequency of a regular confession.

9. If possible, go to confession to the same confessor-priest.

10. Most importantly, cultivate a humble heart by complete obedience to the direction of your confessor. Be patient with yourself. Love is the goal of all our lives. It is important to remember that scrupulosity *usually* (and, quite often, *ultimately*) stems from

one's personal pride and/or arrogance, as though the
scrupulous person holds this opinion about himself:
"I require of myself a higher level of forgiveness and/
or perfection than most normal people."

As to the centrality of the Sacrament of Reconciliation as a target
of misguided scrupulosity, other priests have crafted "10 Commandments for the Scrupulous" of their own. Fr. Santa tells us
that Fr. Don Miller, CSsR, published such a list in 1968. Fr. Santa
produced his own revision in 1996, and revised it in 2013.[17] In Fr.
Santa's latest version, Commandments 1 through 4 focus specifically upon the Sacrament of Reconciliation, while Commandment 7 addresses the need to obey one's confessor.

The scrupulous among us should heed such wise advice that
can transform the Sacrament of Reconciliation from a source of
self-torment to a source of solace, strength, forgiveness, and, as
the *Catechism* tells us, "pardon and peace." To highlight the third
of Fr. Wade's Commandments — regarding doubts of the earnestness of one's sorrow in confession and suggesting the idea
that one's confession was not valid — we would do well to heed
the advice to always consider that our sorrow was sufficient. In
the words of Fr. Kaler, CSsR: "You can't make a bad confession
without knowing you're doing it at the time."[18]

We should take note as well of Father Wade's last bit of advice on the centrality of humility of heart and of obedience in
conquering scrupulosity, echoing advice we've come across earlier in these pages from the likes of Saints Paul, Thomas Aquinas,
Julian of Norwich, and Bl. Henry Suso.

Let's make note of one more of Fr. Wade's insights, this one
from his sixth Commandment regarding setting firm limits on
the amount of time one devotes to examining one's conscience
before confession, and at other times. We are to call to mind our
sins so that we might come to regret them, confess them, and

strive, with God's grace, to avoid them in the future. Still, there is far more than examination of conscience to living a full and loving Christian life imbued with a humble heart. Humility is sometimes said to consist not so much in thinking less of our ourselves, but in thinking of ourselves less. When our thoughts are less focused on every little sin or possible sin *we* have committed, they will be far more open and free to consider the needs of our neighbor, and as the *Catechism* (and Jesus Christ!) tells us, to reconcile ourselves with our brothers.[19]

As the great Church Fathers taught centuries ago, the Sacrament of Penance or Reconciliation provides spiritual healing, serves justice by rendering God and neighbor their rightful due, accepts God's ever-generous mercy, and reopens the free flow of all manners of virtues, gifts, and graces God so loves to rain down on us from heaven. Lord, teach us to cherish it, not fear it!

Anointing of the Sick Can Give Hope to the Scrupulous and Invigorate Body and Soul

We read in James: "Is any man sick among you? Let him bring in the priests of the church, and let them pray over him, anointing him with oil in the name of the Lord. And the prayer of faith shall save the sick man: and the Lord shall raise him up: and if he be in sins, they shall be forgiven him" (5:14–15, Douay-Rheims).

This is the scriptural background for the Sacrament of Anointing of the Sick. This sacrament is most often associated with the Last Rites, when given along with the Sacraments of Reconciliation and Communion (called the *Viaticum* from the Latin meaning "provisions for a journey") to the dying. It was also known as Extreme Unction in the past: *unction* standing for the use of an unguent or oil for anointing, and extreme referring to people who were *in extremis*, or near death.

St. Thomas Aquinas notes that this sacrament does not fail to provide spiritual healing, drawing from divine power, but bodily healing may not follow unless it is required for the spiritual healing in accordance with God's providence. When administered to the dying, this "last anointing" serves as "a preparation for the final journey," and it "fortifies the end of our earthly life like a solid rampart for the final struggles before entering the Father's house" (CCC 1523).

In current practice, one need not be near death to receive this sacrament of hope that drives out fear and restores health and vigor, at least at the spiritual level. The effects of this sacrament on anyone suffering from any manner of illness include special strengthening through the Holy Spirit, "union with the passion of Christ" in which one's suffering "becomes a participation in the saving work of Jesus," and "ecclesial grace" through which the entire Church benefits "through the grace of this sacrament," contributing "to the sanctification of the Church and to the good of all men for whom the Church suffers and offers herself through Christ to God the Father" (CCC 1520–1522).

Modern secular philosophers examining the nature and treatment of scrupulosity have made note of Fr. Santa's use of this sacrament as "a treatment strategy" for scrupulosity.[20] Harking back to our last two sacraments, some scrupulous people fear to partake of the Eucharist even after having received the Sacrament of Reconciliation. This is not what Christ and his Church intended, and if such obsessive thoughts cannot be overcome, one must consider that one's scruples might indeed be a manifestation of obsessive-compulsive disorder. OCD, as we saw, is classified as a mental illness, and therefore, such people "are eligible to have their sins forgiven in the same way as others who are sick, viz., by Anointing of the Sick (or 'Unction')."

This anointing avails them of spiritual healing and should provide psychological solace as well. The worries about whether one did their confession "right" would not apply to this sin-forgiving sacrament in which the grace comes from God through the priest, with no specific words or actions required of the suffering soul. The scrupulous need merely accept the Holy Spirit's strengthening, the union with Christ's passion, and the flow of ecclesial grace.

In short, if you are suffering from serious scrupulosity or have a close loved one who is, you may want to talk over with your priest the possibility of obtaining an Anointing of the Sick.

Holy Orders Give Us Access to All the Sacraments and to God's Prudent Guides

The sacraments we all receive only once, Baptism and Confirmation, leave an indelible seal or mark on our souls, leaving us spiritually transformed by God's holy power. Holy Orders is the sacrament priests receive that provides them with the special indelible seal enabling them to dispense the sacraments to others, acting as Christ upon earth.

Because of this sacrament-dispensing spiritual power, St. Thomas Aquinas said that "Order has more reason for being a sacrament than the others" (*ST*, Supp., q.34, a.3). It's the sacrament that makes possible all the sacraments. Thomas traces this sacrament to Jesus himself: "The apostles received the power of Order before the Ascension (Jn 20:22), where it is said: 'Receive the Holy Ghost.'" In the very next verse, we see that Jesus gave the apostles that power to administer the Sacrament of Reconciliation: "If you forgive the sins of any, they are forgiven; if you retain the sins of any, they are retained" (Jn 20:23). When ordained, priests also receive the chalice and paten in recognition of the power they receive to consecrate the Body and Blood of Christ in that greatest of all sacraments, the Eucharist.

Saint Thomas noted as well that the ancient Church Fathers described one of the functions of Holy Orders as remedying ignorance, making clear that this does *not* mean that the new priest "has his ignorance driven out of him, but that the recipient of Orders is set in authority to expel ignorance among the people" (*ST*, Supp., q.35. a.1). Ignorance means a lack of knowledge, so one of the priest's general roles is to enhance the people's knowledge of the Faith through teaching and preaching, as when giving homilies or organizing catechetical programs for parishioners.

The priest is also in the best position to dispel the special kinds of ignorance that may beset the scrupulous. Perhaps some scruples arise from a simple lack of awareness or gross misinterpretation of Church teachings. Priests can help remedy such ignorance. Still, some scruples arise and persist despite the fact that the sufferer already knows her worries are irrational or her behaviors have not contradicted Church teaching. The ignorance, in this case, is a lack of knowledge about how to overcome admittedly inappropriate scruples. Here too, priests can help. Most priests have encountered people with scruples and have heard their confessions. Some priests, as we've seen in the work of the Redemptorists and others cited within these pages, have special expertise and experience in aiding the scrupulous. If you are suffering from scruples, your own priest may be able to help you himself or refer you to a brother priest whom he knows with special expertise in helping people overcome or cope with spiritual fears and doubts.

When in the throes of scrupulosity, the sufferer has a hard time relying upon his own prudence in making wise, practical moral decisions. We saw that St. Alphonsus Liguori said one's imagination "is a fool" incapable of reason regarding scruples, and in such cases, one should therefore rely on and obey the holy prudence of one's ordained priest. Holy Orders are a literal Godsend to the scrupulous and to us all.

Matrimony: Soul Mates as Sources of Life, of Solace, and Strength

Some people who have been blessed with the Sacrament of Matrimony may bear special crosses from scrupulosity. The cross may be the awareness that one's own scrupulosity is producing unneeded stress for one's spouse, perhaps by constantly seeking his or her reassurance over minor matters, or insisting that things like family prayers be performed in a very precise way and repeated if any "mistakes" are made, yet feeling unable to stop one's own inappropriate expectations, questions, and demands. The cross may be borne by the non-scrupulous spouse who must endure the perpetual questioning or rigid routines.

In such cases, neither spouse should ever forget the virtue and the Holy Spirit's gift of fortitude and the virtues that serve them, like patience and perseverance. The married state can provide serious difficulties and obstacles. Indeed, if I recall correctly, we are warned about things like sickness even as we take our wedding vows! Furthermore, we should heed well these insights from good St. Thomas Aquinas:

> Hence others say that matrimony, inasmuch as it is contracted in the faith of Christ, is able to confer the grace which enables us to do those works which are required in matrimony; and this is more probable, since whenever God gives the faculty to do a thing, He gives also the help whereby man is enabled to make becoming use of that faculty. (*ST*, Supp., q.42. a.3)

Matrimony is a holy sacrament, and the state of marriage itself has always been rooted in natural law. Aristotle, who defined human beings not only as rational animals, but as political animals (social beings who live in a *polis,* or city), even said that "man is an animal more inclined to connubial than political society" (see *ST*, Supp. q.41, a.1),[21] *connubial* indicating the relationship between a man and wife. The Stoic philosopher Musonius Rufus (AD 25–95) recognized that the chief purpose of marriage is that a man and woman will have and raise children together, that marriage is founded upon mutual care and love — indeed "in sickness and in health" — and that the marital bond of partnership and union is admirable and beautiful.[22]

Another great Stoic philosopher, Seneca, disagreed with the philosopher Epicurus, who said that we should cultivate friendships in order to have someone to care for us when *we* are sick, but rather, that we should cultivate friendships in order to have someone we can go to and care for when *they* are sick. Even the pagan Aristotle classed marriage as among the very highest forms of friendship. We are called by nature to be there to help the dear friend and "second self" who is our spouse, even if he or she should suffer with fears and doubts. Through the Sacrament of Matrimony, we are aided by God with the grace and strength required to be there and continue loving and helping our spouse in times of sickness as we look forward to times of health.

Through the Sacrament of Matrimony, those of us who suffer with scruples ourselves are also given strengthening graces by God. God told us from the very beginning that in marriage the husband and wife become as one flesh (see Gn 2:24). A person weighed down by scruples can be lifted up by the spiritual strength of his spouse. Further, if either partner suffers with scruples, marital counseling with a counselor well-versed in the treatment of scrupulosity could be of great benefit for both husband and wife.

In addressing the story of the creation of Eve from one of Adam's ribs, St. Thomas Aquinas recognizes the importance of the symbolic meaning of the passage. Adam's mate was not made from his head, since she was not to rule over him. Neither was she made from his feet, because neither was she to be treated as his lowly slave. Eve was made from Adam's rib to signify their *social union*. Further, "for the sacramental signification; for from the side of Christ sleeping on the Cross, the sacraments flowed

— namely, blood and water — on which the Church was established" (*ST*, I, q.92. a.3).

As the Church, Christ's Bride, flowed from his side, so did God ordain that man's bride would come from his side, to journey with him side by side. When a married person is assailed with spiritual doubts and uncertainties, he or she should rest in the certainty that he or she is not alone in that spiritual battle. One's own spouse and Christ's spouse, the Church, are there to provide reassurance and strength. May God give all married people the grace to journey side by side together to heaven, even if that road should be rocky (or perhaps "pebbly") at times.

Science of Scrupulosity — #5

Wisdom 202: Cognitive-Behavioral Therapy of Scrupulosity

People are disturbed not by things, but by the judgments they make about things.

— Epictetus (*Handbook*, par. 5)

In the broad field of psychotherapy for a variety of mental disorders, cognitive-behavioral therapies are the most commonly used and effective methods today. Most interestingly, the two modern fathers of the methods — psychologist Albert Ellis, Ph.D., founder of Rational-Emotive Behavior Therapy, and psychiatrist Aaron Beck, M.D., founder of Cognitive Therapy — when writing in the 1950s and '60s, both credited a philosopher from the first century A.D. for their fundamental insight into effective therapy.

In the field of psychology, *behaviorism* held sway at the time cognitive therapies were founded. Built upon the foundation of the Russian Ivan Pavlov's work with his famous salivating dogs, and American B. F. Skinner's work with lots of pecking pigeons, the common view was that human mental disturbances were caused by outside stimuli and our reflexive responses (a la Pavlov), or because our own harmful behaviors were somehow "positively reinforced" (rewarded) by others (a la Skinner). In the field of psychiatry, *psychoanalysis* held sway. Built upon the foundation of the work of Sigmund Freud and his cadre of followers, a core tenet was that the disturbances we experience as adults have their roots in experiences we suffered when we were children, buried deep over time in the murky realm of our subconscious.

After spending some years employing the behavioristic and psychoanalytic methods of his day with modest success, Ellis saw that even patients who had apparently gained insight into the childhood origins of their problems often experienced little improvement. For example, a man who discovered something like, "Ah, I lack the desire to work because my workaholic father was so harsh with me!" often remained quite content to remain on the therapist's couch, rather than looking for work. Ellis wrote that, rather than sitting back behind his patients scribbling notes on their early memories and dreams, he would like to sit them up in a chair, look at them face to face, and reason out solutions to their problems — and this he did.

It occurred to Ellis that, even if a person's mental disturbance was originally prompted by some traumatic childhood experience, the reason that person remains traumatized as an adult is because of *what he is telling himself about it today.* He, like Dr. Beck shortly after him, recalled that the Stoic philosophers in general, and Epictetus in particular, clearly taught this powerful lesson thousands of years ago. Different people will handle the same external situations in very different ways. One person may interpret a particular trauma as a reason to give up, while another person may interpret it as a reason to carry on and overcome.

A variation of this idea is also expressed in Scripture. For example: "Count it all joy, my brethren, when you meet various trials, for you know that the testing of your faith produces steadfastness. And let steadfastness have its full effect, that you may be perfect and complete, lacking in nothing" (Jas 1:2–4). Egad! Might even the trials of scrupulosity lead to our eventual perfection?

Various forms of cognitive-behavioral therapies focus on a variety of ways we can change our views, attitudes, and judgments about all manner of distressing things — including scruples. When we have brought our cognition in line with right reason (the goal, come to think of it, of natural moral virtues!), our anxieties will dissolve and our behaviors will improve.

Researchers examining OCD in general have focused on six common "maladaptive OCD-related beliefs":[23]

1. Inflated responsibility
2. Overestimated threat
3. Importance of thought
4. Control of thoughts
5. Perfectionism
6. Intolerance of uncertainty

In brief, the scrupulous may tend to inappropriately exaggerate their own *responsibility* in a variety of ways, perhaps blaming themselves for intrusive thoughts that are triggered by outside circumstances they encounter by accident, or in believing that their own sinful thoughts or behaviors are going to bring great spiritual harm to members of their family.

They may *overestimate threat,* believing, for example, that if they experience an illicit obsessive thought, they will not be able to endure the anxiety that will follow if they do not respond with a ritual compulsion like repetitive prayer or confession. This is one maladaptive belief that the Exposure and Response Prevention (ERP) method takes head on.

They may overestimate the *importance of thoughts,* recalling the phenomenon of "thought-action fusion" we discussed in chapter 1, treating uncontrollable intrusive thoughts as just as bad as immoral acts.

They may also have unrealistic ideas regarding *control of thoughts,* believing that they should have complete control over intrusive thoughts and are sinful when they do not.

Perfectionism is another common belief among the scrupulous, and as every Catholic should know, outside of Jesus Christ and his Mother, not a one of us is without any sin. Indeed, perfectionism is so common among those with OCD and a variety of mental disorders, that I can still hear in my mind the nasally twang of psychologist Albert Ellis from the early 1980s singing one of his Rational-Emotive songs designed to counter it. I can't recall it all, but to the tune of Luigi Denza's humorous "Funiculi Finicula" song,[24] Ellis began by crooning, "Perfect, perfect, rationality! Perfect rationality is the only way for me!" (Indeed, humor and the ability to laugh at oneself can be helpful in battling perfectionism.)

Finally, we again encounter the *intolerance of uncertainty*, recalling that the French (and *The Doubting Disease* author, Dr. Ciarrochi) call scrupulosity itself the "doubting disease."

Sufferers of scruples who consider seeking professional therapy should note that various cognitive methods often incorporated into the treatment of scrupulosity can prove most helpful as well in coping with all sorts of other psychological disturbances too — from depression (Dr. Beck's initial focus) to other anxiety disorders, such as loneliness, anger management, and more.

Saintly Lesson on Scrupulosity — #5

St. Veronica Giuliani (1660–1727)

When she professed as a cloistered nun of the Capuchian Order at Città di Castello in Umbria, Italy, Ursula Giuliani took the name of Saint Veronica, who had wiped the face of Jesus, as we commemorate in the sixth station of the cross. She would go on to be graced by God as one of the Church's greatest mystics, experiencing many dozens of visions, battles with demons, visits by Christ, the Blessed Mother, Saint Augustine, St. Catherine of Siena and other saints, reception of the stigmata, the crown of thorns, and spiritual espousal with Christ.

In obedience to her confessor, she wrote her spiritual experience in a diary that would come to exceed twenty thousand pages![25] Like St. Catherine of Siena and her mystical *Dialogues,* Saint Veronica's *Diaries* would later be published to share her spiritual graces with millions of souls throughout the years. Saint Veronica also had a very special devotion to the Holy Eucharist, and she once proffered profound advice to a scrupulous bishop, who had been tempted with the idea that he should stop saying Mass. She wrote to him as follows in a letter from 1697:

> [Do] not give up celebrating the Holy Mass no matter how much you might have scruples … it is all the work of the tempter so that you will not receive in your soul that Divine Food. Oh, how much I urge you on this point! I would not want one day of your life to go by without receiving this help and support. … It will do you more good than anything else; this is the true medicine for all our ailments; if we are weak It gives us strength, if we are cold, It warms us; if we are afflicted, It consoles us."[26]

She recognized as well the special dignity and grace that comes with the Sacrament of Holy Orders, through which the priest feeds us with that Divine Food of the Eucharist, for "from every priest depends our well-being; each of them should go to celebrate the Mass as clear as crystal."[27]

Her feast day is July 9. St. Veronica Giuliani, pray for us, and pray for our priests, so that we may receive our Divine Food with gratitude and joy.

6

The Power of Pure Prayer (Even If We're Not Paying Attention Very Well!)

*We need to pray to God not in order to make
known to Him our needs or desires but that we
ourselves may be reminded of the necessity of
having recourse to God's help in these matters.*

— St. Thomas Aquinas (*ST*, II-II, q.83, a.2)

*But in the second way we pray to the saints, whether
angels or men, not that God may through them know our
petitions, but that our prayers may be effective through
their prayers and merits. Hence it is written (Apocalypse
8:4) that "the smoke of the incense," namely, "the prayers
of the saints ascended up before God." This is also clear*

from the very style employed by the Church in praying:
since we beseech the Blessed Trinity "to have mercy on
us," while we ask any of the saints "to pray for us."

— St. Thomas Aquinas (*ST*, II-II, q.83, a.4)

Prayer, like the sacraments, can be a source of doubts and fears if misconstrued, but a source of great power, confidence, and solace if embraced and practiced as God intends it. All kinds of scruples may arise surrounding prayer, such as worries about whether one has prayed long enough, said the right prayers at the right times, forgotten someone who had asked for one's prayers, whether one should have said prayers while in a state of sin, if one's prayers "count" if one has lost one's train of thought or, (saints preserve us!) has fallen asleep during prayer. To begin to overcome such scruples, it would behoove us to take a quick look at just what God intends prayer to be before we address such particular concerns.

When St. Thomas Aquinas addresses the seventeen questions posed by article 83 of the *Summa Theologica*'s second part of the second part, he begins early on by citing Cassiodorus (c. AD 485–585, Roman statesman, Christian scholar, and founder of a monastery), who wrote that "prayer (*oratio*) is spoken reason (*oris ratio*)." In prayer we talk to God, and speech is a uniquely human power on earth. Thomas, so precise about everything, explains that animals cannot pray, and when Psalm 147:9 tells us that God gives food to the beasts and the ravens that call to him, it refers to the instinctual desire for God implanted within the animal's souls, and not to actual prayer.

God himself, as God, does not pray because there is nothing he needs from another.[1] Further, prayer is an act of reason that consists in beseeching or requesting things from a superior, and no being is superior to God.

Angels, though intellectual beings like we are, do not reason like we do through step-by-step processes initiated by the information coming in from bodily senses. As spiritual beings, they have no bodies (unless they assume one for special missions from God), and they understand and communicate through an instant illumination from God.

Prayer then, as spoken reason, is the province of only the rational animal — like you and me — and prayer is a most rational thing to do! In fact, Thomas devotes an entire article to explaining why prayer is most *conveniens*, or "becoming" (*ST*, II-II, q.83, a.2).

Thomas notes that prayer starts with and is essentially "the raising up of one's mind to God" and that the "parts" of prayer include *supplications* (humble requests) for particular blessings from God and *thanksgivings* for blessings he has already provided. Another word for supplications is *petitions*, like the seven petitions of the Our Father, that have been summarized as the three "thy" and four "us" petitions. One famous prayer focused on thanks is our blessing before meals. At the risk of oversimplification then, we might say that prayer consists of a whole lot of "Pleases" and "Thank Yous!" to God.

In its simplest sense, prayer is talking to God, as God himself told us to do. Jesus instructed us to go quietly into our rooms, shut the door, and start talking to the Father who will hear us, see us, and reward us (see Mt 6:6). As Saint Thomas made it clear in our opening quotation, God already knows perfectly well both everything you need and everything you will say, but the very act of prayer is itself a reminder to us that he is always there willing to hear and to help us. If our intention is sincere, we need not worry in the slightest whether or not we've "done it right." Do we deny our own children what they need if they ask things from us with imperfect grammar, a stammer, or a lisp?

Of course, God knows our *thoughts* as well as our spoken words, so the Church rightly recognizes the value of spoken vocal prayers, and of silent interior meditative and contemplative forms of prayer through which we seek union with him (see CCC 2700–2724). In contemplative prayer, words may not even be needed: "It is a gaze of faith fixed on Jesus, an attentiveness to the Word of God, a silent love. It achieves real union with the prayer of Christ to the extent that it makes us share in his mystery" (CCC 2724).

Perhaps this calls to mind a beautiful little story told by St. John Vianney (1786–1859). One day the humble parish priest spied an old man sitting in a pew gazing up at the tabernacle and asked him what he was doing. The old man replied, "I look at him and he looks at me." Now, that is a "gaze of faith fixed on Jesus" that totally captures the simple spirit of pure prayer, not as a source of worry or doubt, but of spending quality time, as we might say today, with the Lord Jesus Christ! And if you will forgive some archaic language from days of yore, consider this passage in which St. Thomas Aquinas paraphrases the great Eastern Doctor of the Church, St. John Chrysostom: "Think what happiness is granted thee, what honor bestowed upon thee, when thou conversest with God in prayer, when thou talkest with Christ, when thou askest what thou will, whatever thou desirest" (*ST*, II-II, q.83, a.2). And while you are at it, why not ask him for his aid in overcoming or coping better with your scruples, as it suits his will?

When You Pray You Are Never Truly Alone

Clearly, there is no need to overcomplicate and worry about prayer, our simple heartfelt conversations with God. As for public prayer, during our sacred liturgical rituals, the Mass foremost among them, the structure, sequence, and wording of the prayers have been laid down for us by the Church. Our job is to participate in heart, mind, and soul, in union with the angels and the great communion of saints. We should remember that they are there with us during Mass, praying right along with us — and for us.

Even when we do as Jesus told us, retiring to our rooms, shutting our doors, and praying to our Father, we are never truly alone. God the Father, Son, and Holy Spirit is always with us, while the Blessed Mother and the entire holy family of angels and saints patiently await our invitation to join with us in our prayer. We should remember them and pray to them to intercede for us with God, one of their most cherished duties, so to speak, in heaven.

In our second opening quotation, Thomas Aquinas clarified the saints' role in intercessory prayer for us (a role he himself, as St. Thomas Aquinas, now plays!). We don't need to ask the saints to make sure God knows we are struggling with doubts and fears, for example — since God already knows it — but we may ask the saints to add their prayers for relief to our own, their prayers being like the smoke of the incense that rises to God's altar in heaven. Our *Catechism* describes a wonderful spiritual treasury of merit through which Christ enables the saints to aid fellow Christians on earth and in purgatory. It tells us that "a perennial link of charity exists between the faithful who have already reached their heavenly home, those who are expiating their sins in purgatory and those who are still pilgrims on earth. Between them there is, too, an abundant exchange of all good things" (1475).

The saints are there waiting for us to be asked to pray to God that we may be showered with good things, including relief from scruples. And here is something else to think about. If you worry that you do not pray very well, do you doubt that if you asked the Blessed Mother to help you and pray to God for you, that she would have a pretty good idea of just how to get that done?

There are also a host of other saints you might choose to pray to as well. There are powerful saints especially close to God. St. John the Evangelist, for example, was the "beloved disciple," who reclined upon Jesus' breast at the Last Supper (Jn 13:23). Saint Joseph was, of course, the foster father of Jesus and the earthly head of the Holy Family. You might consider praying to great saints who conquered or endured scrupulosity, like Alphonsus Liguori, Ignatius of Loyola, or other saints featured in our Saintly Lessons for Scrupulous Souls.

St. Thomas Aquinas (who seems to have considered in detail just about everything!) gives us five reasons why we should also sometimes pray to lesser saints who may not sit as close to God in heaven:

1. If a person has a special affinity to a lesser saint, the effects of one's prayers are strengthened by the intensity of one's devotion.
2. We can get bored praying to the same saints all the time, so if we sometimes pray to a different saint, the "fervor of our devotion is aroused anew" (*ST*, Supp., q.72, a.2).
3. Particular saints serve as patrons over particular cases: As we've already mentioned, St. Alphonsus Liguori is the patron of those struggling with scrupulosity itself.
4. It allows us to give the honor that is due to all the saints.
5. The prayers of many saints together may accomplish what the prayers of one alone cannot.

Surely these are excellent reasons to pray to a variety of our brothers and sisters in Christ in heaven! Other saints we might want to pray to include the saint we have chosen for our confirmation name (Mine is Paul. What's yours?). Surely the Angelic Doctor, St. Thomas Aquinas, would also want us to include prayers to the guardian angel assigned to every one of us.[2] Truly we need never be alone when we pray for God's aid for any problems, worries, fears, or doubts!

So, What If You're Not Paying Attention? (or Even Fall Asleep?)

I hope you have seen by now that there is no one right way to pray, but let's take a few minutes to address a few common concerns about prayer mentioned at this chapter's start. One I've considered a time or two myself is the concern that we may have forgotten to pray for particular people who have asked for our prayers, or people we have told we would pray for. Praying for each other is a glorious way to share in the charity that bonds the Mystical Body of Christ. Indeed, my confirmation namesake, Saint Paul, would ask for the prayers of his brothers and sisters in Christ time and again as he wrote to churches in Rome, Corinth, Ephesus, Philippi, Colossae, and Thessalonica.[3] We should certainly follow his example by asking friends and family to pray for us, and by praying for them as well. While we can certainly ask God for the things that we need, the Irish have an old term for prayers focused only on our needs and not on the needs of our neighbor — *stingy prayers*! May we, rather, be generous with our prayers, especially by praying for those who have asked us to pray for them.

Having done master's and doctoral level work specializing in memory, and having written five memory books, I can assure you that nobody's memory is perfect, most certainly including my own! Personally, when praying, I try to recall everyone who has requested my prayers that I can bring to mind, but I also simply ask God to shower his graces on everyone who has asked for my prayers — and everyone who needs them. If you happen to know someone battling scrupulosity, pray to God and the saints that he or she will be open to God's succor. If you yourself are battling doubts and fears about matters of the Faith, consider praying for God's assistance for other scrupulous souls.

Moving right along: Should you dare pray to God if you believe you *may be* in a state of sin? By all means, since such prayer prepares us to receive God's grace. As Fr. L. Miller has reported, "Saint Alphonsus used to say, 'He who prays is saved; he who does not pray is lost.'"[4] If you know for sure you have committed a mortal sin, do go to confession, but do not stop praying in the meanwhile.

Now on to the issues highlighted in our section heading. Since human psychological capacities for sustained attention are as limited and imperfect as our capacities of memory, some people across the centuries have worried that if we become distracted during prayer and lose our train of thought, God will be affronted and will not hear our prayers. Saint Thomas himself addresses this issue squarely in question 83, article 13 of the second part of the second part of his great *Summa Theologica*: "Whether Attention is a Necessary Condition of Prayer?" (Before we dive in, any guesses about his answer?)

Here's the gist of it, hopefully to the relief of any scrupulous among us! "Purposely to allow one's mind to wander in prayer is sinful, and hinders the prayer from having fruit. ... But to wander in mind unintentionally does not deprive the prayer of fruit."

Thomas, being Thomas, also gets much more precise, listing three main *effects* of prayer:

1. **Merit**, which comes from all acts inspired by the love of God
2. **Impetration**, the production of petitions or requests to God
3. **Spiritual refreshment** of the mind of one who prays

For the first two effects, simply the initial intention to pray is sufficient, even if attention is lost, given that one must have begun with the intention to persevere in prayer. For the last, the immediate effect of spiritual refreshment of the mind comes only while paying attention. That God desires to refresh our spirits should discourage us from setting up excessive demands on ourselves for extended prayers or unnecessary repetitions that will likely exceed our limited abilities to maintain focus.

But what exactly should we focus on during prayers? Thomas, again being Thomas, has provide us some answers. He describes three kinds of attention we can bring to vocal prayer:

1. Attention to the *words* so we say them correctly.
2. Attention to the *meanings* of the words.
3. Attention to the end or goal of the prayer — that is, to God!

Thomas explains that even the slow-witted who cannot remember or understand the words of certain prayers are still able, within their limits, to raise their thoughts to God. Further, even among the learned and holy, "this attention, whereby the mind is fixed on God, is sometimes so strong that the mind forgets all other things" (*ST*, II-II, q.83, a.13).

Just think about this for a minute. Who is more aware than God himself of the limitations of our fallen human nature, short attention spans and all? "For he knows our frame; / he remembers that we are dust" (Ps 103:14). God appreciates the fact that we try to pray, even when our wandering minds go astray!

Yes, but … what if you actually *fall asleep* while praying? Well then, you are in some very good company! Saint Dominic, who would sometimes pray into the night, was found by his friars face down on the church pavement one night — fast asleep! St. Thérèse of Lisieux wrote of her own tendency toward drowsiness when praying the Liturgy of the Hours, but it did not upset or deter her.

And here is perhaps my favorite story about a sleepy saint. Can you imagine hearing the great Saint Patrick, patron of Ireland, preaching live at a great assembly — and falling asleep right in front of him? Well, an ancient hagiography (saint's biography) of St. Brigid of Kildare, patroness of Ireland, says she did just that!

As the legend has it, Patrick himself had come to Clogher in Findermore, in the province of Ulster in the northeast of Ireland, to preach on the Gospels for three days and nights without ceasing. While neither Patrick nor his audience grew weary, who should be found fast asleep but the young abbess, Brigid herself. Patrick chided her when she awoke, but she asked forgiveness saying, "O Father, forgive me; O most pious Lord, spare me, for during this hour I have had a vision."[5] Brigid then reported that she saw four ploughs that were plowing all of Ireland, while sowers in white garments scattered seed. Corn stalks rose up in an instant and ripened, while rivulets of fresh milk filled the furrows. Then other ploughmen clothed in black appeared and destroyed the corn with their ploughshares. They planted tares instead, and these filled the furrows.

Patrick replied that Brigid had seen a true and wondrous vision from God. Those clad in white and plowing the field were Brigid, Saint Patrick himself, and their disciples, planting the seeds of God's word from the Gospels throughout every province in Ireland. (In fact, so successful were Patrick and Brigid that Ireland itself would soon become known as the "Island of Saints and Scholars.") The rivers poured forth the milk of Christian faith resulting from their labors. Those in black would be bad teachers who would come later, nearer the end of the time, seeking to destroy their holy work and nearly seducing the whole of mankind.

Well, it has been around fifteen centuries since Patrick and Brigid joined God in heaven, and we can only wonder if those ploughmen clothed in black have arrived among us today. Furthermore, while few of us who fall asleep in the midst of a prayer or a homily are likely to be blessed with a vision from God, we can rest assured — pardon the pun — that God still loves us and watches over us as we sleep, just as our parents did when we were little.

As a parting thought, when I write a book, I tend to keep an editor (sometimes several) pretty busy, as they rightly review my work for all my mistakes and verbal infelicities, and then try to figure out how they can clean things up. And I thank God for them! Praying, however, is a world apart from formal writing. There are no verbal typos. God does not want footnotes, endnotes, or flowery phrases. He does not care if you accidentally misspell words (well, mispronounce, I suppose), or if you borrow the words of others, as in our vast treasury of traditional Catholic prayers.

God wants you to know him and love him, particularly in the awesome reality that "God is love" (1 Jn 4:16), and that he so loved us "that he gave his only-begotten Son, that whoever believes in him should not perish but have eternal life" (Jn 3:16). He wants not to condemn us, but to save us (see Jn 3:17). God does not need many or precisely perfect words from us. What he wants is a simple, heartfelt conversation with one of his children.

Let's hark back again to St. John Chrysostom's wise and inspiring words, paraphrased this time, in more modern language: "Think what happiness is granted you, what honor bestowed upon you, when you converse with God in prayer, when you talk with Christ, when you ask what you will, whatever you desire" (*ST*, II-II, q.83, a.2). Just think about it! (And pray!)

Science of Scrupulosity — #6

Wisdom 303: When You Know Your ACTs and DBTs Scrupulosity May Flee

> *One recent study found that treatment with*
> *ACT was clinically helpful in 46–66% of the*
> *sample after 8 one-hour treatments at the*
> *3-month follow-up mark post-treatment. ...*
>
> *Occasionally, if CBT, ERP, and ACT are not effective,*
> *some sufferers seek out other treatments like*
> *Dialectical Behavior Therapy (DBT), Eye Movement*
> *Desensitization and Reprocessing (EMDR) and more.*
>
> — Kyle N. Weir, Ph.D., LMFT[6]

Those who might consider professional therapy to help cope with scrupulosity should be aware that some therapists and counselors, especially those who specialize in the treatment of OCD, have many tools in their toolboxes to help dissemble scruples. We saw that Exposure and Response Prevention treatment is a gold-standard treatment designed with OCD in mind, and that cognitive-behavioral methods, the gold-standard of psychotherapy in general, can also be mined for ideas and techniques that can help cure scruples. In this essay I'll simply point out a few other popular psychological treatment methods that have been used with some success on scrupulosity.

The ACT of our quotation above refers to Acceptance and Commitment Therapy (pronounced as the word "act" by its practitioners). First written about in book form in 1999, ACT is a well-researched and widely-used method of therapy for a variety of disorders, which some therapists use to treat OCD. As we saw in the quotation, in at least one study, it proved effective for about one-half to two-thirds of the clients even three months after the treatment ended. Highly respected by many practitioners in the field, its most prominent handbook, *Acceptance and Commitment Therapy: The Process and Practice of Mindful Change,* was published in a second edition over twenty years later.[7] Designed to encourage "psychological flexibility," rather than the mental rigidity often characteristic of mental distress, it aims at six key processes: defusion, acceptance, attention to the present moment, self-awareness, values, and committed action.

Another method of psychotherapy some therapists employ with OCD/scrupulosity patients is known as Dialectical Behavior Therapy (DBT). A particular version of cognitive-behavior therapy first designed for treatment of the clinically difficult and usually longstanding Borderline Personality Disorder, it has been adapted for use in other self-destructive or anxiety-producing disorders like eating disorders, addictions, Post-Traumatic Stress Disorder, and OCD. It also has features overlapping with ACT, including its focus on mindfulness, living in the present moment, and growing in awareness of the information coming in from the senses and of one's emotional states before engaging in compulsive behaviors.[8]

Another interesting and well-researched approach, developed by neuropsychiatrist Jeffery M. Scwhartz, M.D., is detailed in his *Brain Lock: Free Yourself from Obsessive-Compulsive Behavior.* He details research showing what goes on in the brain when people experience obsessions and compulsions (including findings regarding particular brain structures called the *caudate nucleus* and the *putamen* deep within the brain), and, more importantly, what we can do about it. He details four key steps in what are essentially cognitive-behavioral techniques:

1. **Relabel** — For example, when a disturbing intrusive thought arises, one trains oneself not to take it at face value, but to name it for what it is, as in "This thought is an *obsession*; this urge is a *compulsive* urge."[9]

2. **Reattribute** — Dr. Schwartz sums it up in one simple phrase we can say to ourselves regarding scruples: "It's not me — it's my OCD."[10] This can help us remember that obsessions and compulsive urges are false and meaningless, and we need not heed them.

3. **Refocus** — In this step, one tries to bypass the actions of some of those deep brain structures that focus attention by shifting one's attention away from the obsession or compulsion to some other positive behavior. This could be as simple as taking a walk, reading a book, or engaging in some pleasant hobby.

4. **Revalue** — In the fourth and final step, we build upon the previous steps that have reconstrued ideas and urges such as scruples as false alarms (false impressions in Stoic/Epictetan terms), as biochemical imbalances occurring in the brain that need not be heeded and can be altered. Dr. Schwartz suggests the use of a concept called the "Impartial Spectator" here, in which we imagine ourselves as objective spectators of our own thoughts and behaviors, remaining calm and being better able to give ourselves good advice.

Of course, I've merely provided the simplest of introductions to a few of the methods commonly used to treat OCD, including the "religious subtype" that we call scrupulosity. Are you interested in learning more about such therapies on your own, or going through them with a therapist? Should you be interested in doing so? We'll address both questions in our last Science of Scrupulosity essay, right after Christ himself takes center stage in our chapter 7.

Saintly Lesson for Scrupulous Souls — #6

St. Maximilian Kolbe (1894–1941)

St. Maximilian Kolbe is another saint who battled against scrupulosity, and who also strikes a personal chord with me. At the time our younger son went through his confirmation classes, he was greatly impressed by the story of an incident during World War II at the infamous Auschwitz concentration camp. The Nazis had gathered a group of men at random as a punishment for prisoners who had tried to escape. These men were to be starved to death. When an innocent man with a wife and family was chosen, a Catholic priest volunteered to take his place, and did. That priest was Fr. Maximilian Kolbe, a Polish Conventual Franciscan friar. This story is why our Kyle's confirmation name is Maximilian.

Father Kolbe has become one of the most loved and revered of our modern saints. A highly intelligent man who would obtain doctorates in both philosophy and theology, at the age of twelve he experienced a vision of the Virgin Mary. She carried two crowns: a white one symbolizing virginity and a red one symbolizing martyrdom. When she asked which crown he preferred, he replied that he wanted both. With his powerful devotion to the Blessed Mother, he started the Militia Immaculata (Army of the Immaculate One) to convert unbelievers through the intercession of the Blessed Mother. He would become a prolific publisher and would establish monasteries in India and in Japan.

One of his patronages is for drug addicts, and he is sometimes pictured with a needle in his arm. This is because when he did not die after several days of starvation, the Nazis injected him with carbolic acid to hasten his death.

Saint Kolbe's life and death should inspire all of us, and especially the scrupulous, since he was reported to battle against scruples in his youth. So severe were his scruples at one time that his religious superior assigned a brother friar to accompany him at all times, so Kolbe could report to that priest whenever he had a troubling thought, and receive from him priestly guidance. Again, we see humility, docility, and obedience in action as remedies to scrupulosity. That Father Kolbe possessed and used the Holy Spirit's gifts as well was made clear in the supernatural fortitude that allowed him to lay down his life for a stranger.

The one spiritual lesson that always comes first to my mind when I ponder this great saint is his famous mathematical formula of sorts that runs as follows: $V + v = S$, where capital V stands for God's will (*voluntas* being Latin for "will"), small v stands for our will, and S stands for sanctity. An even simpler formula is $V = v$ (perhaps easier still if we translate it into English as $W = w$). We should strive to make our own wills match the will of God. If our minds are set upon prayerfully knowing God's will, and our hearts and wills are set upon acting it out, our souls will be too busy focusing on what matters the most to find time to quibble over our own trifles.

His feast day is August 14. St. Maximilian Kolbe, pray for us that we might acquire the humility, docility, obedience, and courage to align our will with God's will and cast our scruples aside.

7

Christ Loves All Who Are Burdened and Yearns to Lighten Their Yokes

Come to me, all who labor and are heavy laden, and I will give you rest. Take my yoke upon you, and learn from me; for I am gentle and lowly in heart, and you will find rest for your souls. For my yoke is easy, and my burden is light.

— Matthew 11:28–30

Yes, his yoke is easy and his burden light: therefore you will find rest for your souls. This yoke does not oppress but unites; this burden has wings, not weight. This yoke is charity. This burden is brotherly love.

— St. Aelred of Rievaulx[1]

In chapter 3, we examined the two scriptural laws. The Law of Moses was God's first covenant with fallen man, a good law indeed, but a law marked with fear, subservience, earthly rewards, and heavy burdens upon the soul. But after "the Word became flesh and dwelt among us" (Jn 1:14), and the Virgin Mary bore a son named "Jesus," who would be called "Son of the Most High" (Lk 1:31–32), Jesus Christ, through his life, passion and resurrection, would fulfil the Old Law and established the new Law, marked by love rather than fear, freedom rather than subservience, eternal rather than temporal rewards — a law laying light rather than heavy burdens upon our souls. In this chapter, we'll examine the Lawgiver himself and the love and forgiveness he shares with every one of us.

Perhaps some fans of comic books or sci-fi movies will be familiar with the fictional character Judge Dredd. An unforgiving law enforcement officer in a dystopic future, his role was that of a police officer, judge, jury, and executioner, all in one. His most famous (or infamous) line was: "I *am* the law!" Well, of all who have walked or will walk the earth, only Jesus Christ could rightly declare "I *am* the Law!" as he declared that he is the "way, and the truth, and the life" (Jn 14:6). Christ is indeed the ultimate judge as well.

The Church teaches that, when we die, we will each undergo a "particular judgment" from God, which will determine whether our souls will reside in heaven, hell, or purgatory (CCC 1021–1022). This is when we are judged as individual persons. Later, at the time of the last, final, or general judgment, our bodies will be resurrected, gathered together, and Jesus will come again in glory, accompanied by angels to publicly judge all who have lived, after which we will reside eternally, body and soul, in heaven or hell (see CCC 1038–1041, building on scriptural verses, including Mt 25:31–46 and Jn 5:28–29). This is when we are judged as members of the human race.

So, Jesus is indeed the ultimate judge, but a judge we should never dread, since he loves us dearly and wants to judge us as innocent, so that we may spend eternity with him. This is why he sent us the Holy Spirit, who showers us with God's graces during our time here on earth. Unfortunately, many people battling scruples tend to needlessly dread Christ's judgment by zooming in and focusing on the instances reported in the Gospels where Jesus rebuked people and made what may seem to be harsh judgments, while downplaying his overwhelming lessons and actions of forgiveness and mercy.[2] Rather, we should recall that his rebukes were typically directed at scribes, Pharisees, and hypocrites who had imposed unnecessary burdens upon others, making their burdens unnecessarily heavy and encouraging scruples about trivial things, like "tith[ing] mint and dill and cumin," while neglecting "the weightier matters of the law, justice and mercy and faith," thereby "straining out a gnat and swallowing a camel" (Mt 23:23–24). Scruples, we might say, make not only mountains out of pebbles, but camels out of gnats!

When Jesus mentions law and justice, mercy and faith are there as well, in the very same sentence. Furthermore, when asked about the greatest commandment of all, he answered — building upon the words of Deuteronomy 6:4–5 and Leviticus 19:18 — that first we are to love God with all that we are, and second to love our neighbor as ourselves (see Mt 22:35–40; Mk 12:28–34; Lk 10:27). These great commandments of love were present even in the Old Law, yet people like the Pharisees smothered them in a bewildering plethora of petty rules and laws like a great big pile of very small scruples.

Consider, for example, how the Pharisees laid in wait for Jesus so they might publicly chide him for violating the Third Commandment of keeping holy the Sabbath Day by healing a man with a withered hand. How did Jesus react to their obsession over keeping the apparent letter of that Law while ignoring its loving spirit? Jesus asked them, "Is it lawful on the sabbath to do good or to do harm, to save life or to kill?" Then he said to the man, "Stretch out your hand" and his hand was healed (see Mk 3:4–5; Mt 12:9–14).

And this was not the only time Jesus would supposedly violate the Sabbath in the eyes of the Pharisees. For another example, he straightened the back of a woman who had been bent over with "a spirit of infirmity" for a full eighteen years, again to the scandal of the Pharisees (see Lk 13:10–17).

Jesus taught that the spirit of loving charity that underlies God's laws matters infinitely more than petty, restrictive, man-made rules. Who in their right mind would not pull one of their sheep out of a pit (see Mt 12:11) or lead their ox or donkey to water (Lk 13:15) on the Sabbath Day?

We should note well that in both of these cases, neither the man nor the woman was reported to have approached Jesus, but rather he sought them out to heal them. We are the lost sheep, the thirsty oxen and donkeys, whom Jesus comes to save and to nourish with the water of life. He is always calling to us to be saved and refreshed, if we but heed his call, even on the Sabbath Day (in fact, especially so during Mass!).

In his Sermon on the Mount, Jesus preached, "So whatever you wish that men would do to you, do so to them; for this is the law and the prophets" (Mt 7:12). Notice the positive, proactive nature of this golden rule. We are not merely told not to do bad things to people, but to go out of our way to do good things for them. When we find ourselves spending more time trying to figure out good things we can do for our family, friends, and neighbors (in imitation of Christ himself), we may find ourselves with precious little time and energy to worry about whether or not we may have accidentally committed some sin that the Pharisees would find far more interesting than Christ would.

Recall too that Jesus did not merely *speak* of mercy to imperfect sinners, but he *lived* it again and again. He warned us in that mountain sermon to root out lust from our hearts and souls, but when confronted with the many-times-married Samaritan woman at the well, he revealed to her that he is the Messiah, and her testimony brought many Samaritans to Christ (see Jn 4:1– 42). When the Pharisees brought Jesus the woman caught in the act of adultery, citing the Law of Moses dictating that she must be stoned, he wrote with his finger on the ground, and said, "Let him who is without sin among you be the first to throw a stone at her" (Jn 8:7). If I recall correctly, G. K. Chesterton suggested that perhaps Jesus scribbled names quite familiar to some Pharisees present who'd had first-hand familiarity with that particular sin. In any event, the Pharisees went away and Jesus showed mercy to the adulteress, saying, "Neither do I condemn you; go, and do not sin again" (Jn 8:11). He offers the same mercy to each of us for any of our sins. We need merely repent and do our best to commit real sins no more (and to repent of them again and again if we do, even "seventy times seven" — an unlimited number of times) (Mt 18:22).

Jesus' forgiveness and mercy are in action throughout the course of his social ministry as described in all four Gospels, and continued even as he was nailed to the cross, and breathed his last words before experiencing and conquering death. Of the seven famous phrases or "last words of Jesus on the cross" that appear in the four Gospels, the first is "Father, forgive them; for they know not what they do" (Lk 23:34).[3] Jesus, in the midst of his agony, asks his heavenly Father to forgive the very people who nailed him to the cross. Can we seriously think he would not ask his Father to forgive us the petty sins we fear we just might have committed?

His boundless, loving mercy is seen in the second of the seven last words as well: "Truly I say to you, today you will be with me in Paradise." Recall that these words were spoken to a common thief, whom we now call the good thief, the penitent thief, or Saint Dismas. At the very end of his life, unlike the other criminal who berated Jesus, Saint Dismas chided the belligerent criminal, then turned to Jesus and said, "Jesus, remember me when you come in your kingly power" (Lk 23:40–42). And we know he is now a saint in heaven, since Jesus replied to him, "Truly, I say to you, today you will be with me in Paradise" (Lk 23:43).

Come to think of it, what a powerful little prayer to say — and say only *once,* just like the good thief — when struggling with a scrupulous thought: "Jesus, remember me when you come in your kingly power!" You can rest assured that Christ the King will not forget you!

The Yoke's on You (Thanks Be to God!)

Jesus told us that his yoke is easy and his burden light, and he invited *all* who labor and are heavy-laden to come to him for rest. There is no reason we need to heap piles of pebbles upon our own necks and backs.

Saint Aelred explained that Jesus' yoke is light because it is the yoke of love. Like the wings of faith and reason, Christ's yoke itself has wings to bear us to heaven. The burden we bear is brotherly love (and as far as burdens go, who could ask for a better one?).

Saint Thomas explained that the light yoke of the Law of Jesus replaced the heavy yoke of Moses, made heavier yet by the Pharisees.

St. John Chrysostom waxed eloquent[4] on Jesus' yoke of love as follows: "He said not, Come ye, this man and that man, but All whosoever are in trouble, in sorrow, or in sin, not that I may exact punishment of you, but that I may remit your sins. Come ye, not that I have need of your glory, but that I seek your salvation. 'And I will refresh you;' not, I will save you, only; but that is much greater, 'I will refresh you,' that is, I will set you in all quietness."[5]

Are you troubled? Are you sad? Do you fret that you have sinned (or may have done so)? Then *you* are the man or woman Jesus calls out to, that he might still all your sorrows and worries, forgive all your sins, and refresh you with the waters of eternal life. Christ's whole life on earth was about you, me, and every one of us. He came so that we might share abundant life (Jn 10:10), not a life of worry and doubt.

Let's end by giving good Saint Thomas a chance to wax eloquent too with some words of his own from *Verbum Supernum Prodiens,* "The Word from Heaven Now Proceeding," among the prayers Thomas was commissioned to write for the new feast of Corpus Christi. The Angelic Doctor sums up Christ's mission to each of us in beautiful verse:

> Being born, He became our friend.
> At supper, He became our food.
> Dying, He was our ransom's price
> And reigning, is our eternal good.[6]

Science of Scrupulosity — #7

Wisdom 404: Knowledge is Power — Scrupulosity Resources

Wise men lay up knowledge.

— Proverbs 10:14

Wise men and women lay up knowledge. Philosopher Francis Bacon was right when he wrote that "knowledge is power," building upon yet another verse from Proverbs (see 24:5): "A wise man is mightier than a strong man, and a man of knowledge than he who has strength." If we set our minds toward *doing* something, it is of the greatest importance that we know *how* to do it, and this includes curing or coping with scrupulosity.

We've encountered plenty of wisdom from philosophers, saints, and psychologists in these pages, but I'd like to end these Science of Scrupulosity essays with advice on where to go to store up more helpful knowledge. I'll begin by taking cues from two great men of faith, Ezekiel and Saint Jerome: "And he said to me, 'Son of man, eat this scroll that I give you and fill your stomach with it.' Then I ate it; and it was in my mouth as sweet as honey" (Ez 3:3). As Saint Jerome comments, "Eating the book is the starting-point of reading and of basic history. When, by diligent meditation, we store away the book of the Lord in our memorial treasury, our belly is filled spiritually and our guts are satisfied."[7]

Gobbling up good books nourishes our minds and souls. First and foremost for all Christians are the books of Scripture, which we should feast upon daily. For those of us battling scrupulosity (or who have loved ones, parishioners, or clients who are), it may well behoove us to satisfy our appetites by consuming additional books, so that "our belly is filled spiritually and our guts are satisfied" in the graphic imagery of Jerome, the very saint who translated the Holy Scriptures themselves into Latin.

Therefore, I'd like to provide a small but delicious menu of books on scrupulosity from which you might choose to dine sometime. I will arrange these recommended readings alphabetically by author's name and in accordance with our theme of twin wings of faith and reason (or science), bearing in mind that in a few of them, both wings flap vigorously. Finally, I will suggest some other resources that might help you fly beyond scrupulosity. Let's begin.

Scrupulosity on the Wing of Faith

Scruples and Sainthood: Accepting and Overcoming Scruples with the Help of the Saints
Trent Beattie, Loreto Publications, 2010

I highly recommend this book on the spiritual dimensions of scrupulosity and what we can do about it. It is full of insightful and inspirational quotations from a variety of saints. It also addresses many of the issues we have touched on in these pages: the virtues, temptations, prayer, the Sacraments of Reconciliation and the Eucharist. Finally, it provides a special focus on how other great blessings of the Catholic Faith — from the power of intercessory prayer to the Blessed Mother, to the use of sacramentals like holy water and the rosary — can help us battle scrupulosity and turn earthly suffering into a heavenly beatitude.

The Doubting Disease: Help for Scrupulosity and Religious Compulsions
Joseph W. Ciarrochi, Paulist Press, 1999

As mentioned in our chapter 1, this book flies on the wings

of both faith and reason, written by a psychologist who had once been a Catholic priest. It is a terse but comprehensive look at scrupulosity from multiple angles, including the history of its conceptualization, and its psychological and spiritual treatment. It can also be used as a self-help book and includes charts that can be used to construct one's own scrupulosity exposure hierarchies to employ the Exposure and Response Avoidance method.

Spiritual Director and Physician: The Spiritual Treatment of Sufferers from Nerves and Scruples
Rev. Fr. Victor Raymond, O.P., Forgotten Books, 2012

Don't be fooled by the 2012 publication date. Forgotten Books republished this book, which was originally published in 1914, rightly recognizing that it should not be forgotten. I find it a fascinating "old school" approach to scrupulosity with the kind of deep knowledge and devout faith I've come to expect from Dominican authors in the tradition of St. Thomas Aquinas. Beginning with a laudatory preface from a leading psychiatrist of Fr. Raymond's acquaintance, the book moves on to address the nature and the psychological and spiritual dimensions of scrupulosity as understood at that time. Readers will find that, even more than a century ago, the understanding of those dimensions was quite good. The book's first part includes chapters on common mental disorders of the time: neurosis, hysteria, and psychasthenia (involving obsessions and disorders of physical movement or pain), while the book's second part zooms in on scruples. It gives us an idea of the state of the Church and of psychiatry more than a century ago, and it abounds with timeless insights from Scripture, Church Fathers, Doctors of the Church, and sundry saints.

Searching for and Maintaining Peace
Fr. Jacques Phillipe, Alba House, 2002 & Scepter, 2012

I once had the pleasure of speaking at the same conference with Fr. Phillipe, who amused and inspired the audience despite the need for an English language interpreter. People battling scrupulosity have reported his books as foundational in uprooting tendencies toward scrupulosity.

The Holy Gospels
by Matthew, Mark, Luke, and John

Repeated reflection on the mercy and love of Jesus Christ revealed in Scripture can provide a healing balm to the soul. Some scrupulous souls have noted the soothing power of Christ's words in Matthew 6:25–34, where he tells us not to be anxious about *anything* in our lives, but rather to trust in God who cares for the needs of even the birds of the air and lilies of the field. Jesus does not want us to worry. He would rather we experience the peace he can bring our souls through his words in Scripture, his mystical presence in the Eucharist, and through the Holy Spirit dwelling within us. Chapters 14–16 in John's Gospel also provide us powerful insights into Jesus Christ as he truly is, and not as we might fashion him out of our unnecessary doubts and fears. Indeed, we should never forget the words with which these beautiful chapters begin and end: "Let not your hearts be troubled; believe in God, believe also in me" (Jn 14:1), and, "I have said this to you, that in me you may have peace. In the world you have tribulation; but be of good cheer, I have overcome the world" (Jn 16:33). St. Jerome warned us, "Ignorance of Scripture is ignorance of Christ." We are certainly not all called to be biblical scholars like Jerome was, but developing a habit of spending a few minutes with the Gospels on a regular basis can help bring us the peace the Prince of Peace promised us.

Scrupulosity on the Wing of Reason (or Science)

I cited at times from some clinical handbooks that may be of interest to any therapists or counselors who come across these pages. David A. Clark's *Cognitive-Behavioral Therapy for OCD and Its Subtypes* (Guilford, 2020) is a comprehensive guide to modern cognitive-therapy approaches, with appraisal of the research literature, a thorough chapter detailing the Exposure and Response Prevention method, and a chapter on "Sex, Harm, and Religious Obsessions." Another excellent professional resource with contributions from multiple clinicians and a chapter devoted to scrupulosity is Jonathan Abramowitz, Dean McKay, and Steven Taylor's (eds.) *Clinical Handbook of Obsessive-Compulsive Disorder and Related Problems* (John Hopkins University Press, 2008). As for psychological books of possible interest to general readers, I'll recommend two below.

Daring to Challenge OCD: Overcome Your Fear of Treatment & Take Control of Your Life Using Exposure & Response Prevention
Joan Davidson, Ph.D. (foreword by Jeff Bell), New Harbinger Publications, 2014

This book provides an easily understandable and detailed description of Exposure and Response Prevention with instruction on just how it is used in therapy. Though it addresses OCD in general, of the three case studies presented in detail, one of them was a former priest who battled with scrupulosity.

Brain Lock: Free Yourself from Obsessive-Compulsive Behavior, 20th Anniversary Edition
Jeffery M. Schwartz, M.D. with Beverly Beyette, Harper Perennial, 2016

Dr. Schwartz's method was described in brief in our last chapter's Science of Scrupulosity essay. Though the book addresses OCD in general and does not specifically focus on scrupulosity, I recommend this as an excellent resource for the layperson battling scrupulosity or with a loved one who is. It is engagingly written and includes interesting neuroscientific findings about brain structures and pathways that tend to foster and perpetuate obsessions and compulsions. Though Dr. Schwartz stresses the involvement of brain structures and processes in obsessions and compulsions, he in no way implies that the sufferer's brain is irrevocably damaged and that one must just learn to live with it. Indeed, his whole premise is that there are simple, effective ways that, through changing our thoughts and behaviors, will "unlock" our brains and free us of unneeded fears, doubts, and anxiety. I briefly mentioned his "four Rs" of Relabel, Reattribute, Refocus, and Revalue, but he explains them in greater detail and shows how they can also enhance Exposure and Response Prevention methods. Its popularity is attested to by the publication of a twentieth anniversary edition!

Finally, I'll note that there are also many other potentially helpful and easily accessible resources to help cope with scrupulosity. The phenomenon is so widespread that if you type keywords like "Catholic scrupulosity" into an internet search bar, you are going to find many useful articles written by people suffering from it, and contributions from Catholic authors associated with a number of prominent Catholic publishers. To start you off with an excellent example, I recommend an insightful piece from Rhonda Ortiz,[8] who also runs the Scripture for the Scrupulous newsletter.[9]

Saintly Lesson for Scrupulous Souls — #7

St. Francis de Sales (August 21, 1567– December 28, 1622)

It did not even occur to me when I chose him for this last essay, but here we have lessons from yet another saint with a personal connection of sorts, for St. Francis de Sales is the patron saint of … Catholic writers! And for the best of reasons. Though I do not recall stories of this wonderful saint battling his own scrupulosity, this grace-filled bishop and spiritual director crafted letters and books that have, for the last four hundred years, provided solace to the scrupulous and inspiration to all people who desire to live a devout life.

If those last words ring a bell, it is because his *Introduction to the Devout Life,* first published in 1608, remains among the best (if not *the* best) spiritual guides for lay people living lives full of duties and worries out in the world. He also came to my mind because virtually every book I pick up on scrupulosity quotes words of wisdom from this remarkable saint. Hence, I think it best if I keep my own words to a minimum and treat you to a mini-feast of the saintly lessons (and delightfully homey imagery) of our own champion in heaven, St. Francis de Sales:

> One of the first applications of gentleness is to prac-tice it toward ourselves. We ought not to become overly disturbed with ourselves because of our imperfections. Even though it is natural for us to be displeased and confused when we commit faults, we must guard against too strong a disappointment, chagrin and anger because of them. Many are at fault in this: they become enraged at being angry, disturbed at being disturbed and vexed at being vexed![10]

Do like little children who hold onto their father with one hand while gathering strawberries with the other. While working with one hand on earthly affairs, always hold the hand of your heavenly Father with the other, turning toward Him from time to time to see if He approves the conduct of your affairs and occupations.[11]

Whenever you perceive that you are tempted … do as children do when they see a wolf or a bear. They immediately run to the protection of father or mother, or at least cry out to them for help. Do you have recourse in the same way to God, calling for His mercy and help. This is the remedy taught us by Our Lord Himself: "Pray that you enter not into temptation."[12]

His feast day is January 24. St. Francis de Sales, pray for us that we may hold and trust in the strong hand of our Father as we pursue the devout life with our earthly and heavenly family.

Conclusion

Waiting in Joyful Hope

"Peace I leave with you; my peace I give to you; not as the world gives do I give to you. Let not your hearts be troubled, neither let them be afraid.

— John 14:27

Well, we've opened up our wings of the Catholic Faith and of science-backed reason to fly to firm truths about the "doubting disease" and also about ourselves. So, is scrupulosity a cross that you bear, or perhaps a cross born by a loved one close to you? If so, hopefully you have found encouragement or at least some measure of solace knowing that perhaps scrupulosity will be overcome, and if not, then at least lightened and made a little easier to bear.

We should know without the slightest doubt that Christ does not want us to live this life with troubled hearts mired in fear.

Rather, the Prince of Peace freely offers peace of mind, heart, and soul to us all. He told us so himself! Some of us, perhaps due to some sort of misfiring in our brains, will find it much harder to find such peace on earth than others. Still, our lessons from modern psychology and from the timeless wisdom of the Church can provide hope that with diligent thought and effort — on one's own for some, and under the care of a counselor, confessor, or spiritual director for others — a greater measure of peace can be obtained during our relatively brief stay on earth.

Of course, Jesus told us he gives us peace "not as the world gives." We can embrace the hope that our ultimate peace and ultimate bliss will be found eternally with him in heaven. This is why God gave us the virtues to fight against sins, the Holy Spirit's gifts to strengthen us in our battles, and the Sacraments to help us stand taller and firmer against real sin, and to get right back up when we do fall.

But what if our scruples are not so easily removed from our souls? What if certain doubts linger, if undesirable thoughts still sometimes pop into our minds, and we feel we must *do* something about them — *right now?*

In that case, heed well the spiritual wisdom of that wonderful mystic, Bl. Henry Suso, who said:

> We may conclude that persons who suffer from scruples are the most favored by divine love, and the most certain of reaching heaven when they bear this trial in patience and humility. Scrupulous souls die continually, they suffer a continual purgatory, and so they leave the earth to fly to heaven purified and free from sins to expiate.

Like St. Thomas Aquinas before him, Blessed Henry was a friar of Saint Dominic's Order of Preachers. Early in the magnificent *Summa Theologica,* Thomas counters a common argument against the existence of God, namely the objection that if an infinitely good God exists, there could be no evil in the world; but we all know darn well that our world abounds in evil. Some call this "the problem of evil." Thomas replies by quoting from St. Augustine of Hippo's *Handbook:* "Since God is the highest good, He would not allow any evil to exist in His works, unless His omnipotence and goodness were such as to bring good even out of evil." Thomas then concludes: "This is part of the infinite goodness of God, that He should allow evil to exist, and out of it produce good" (*ST*, I, Q. 2, a.3).

Let's return now to Blessed Henry. Those suffering from scrupulosity should not despair if their scruples never seem to leave them completely at peace. As Saint James told us: "Count it all joy, my brethren, when you meet various trials, for you know that the testing of your faith produces steadfastness. And let steadfastness have its full effect, that you may be perfect and complete, lacking in nothing" (Jas 1:2–5).

Scruples themselves, and our efforts to overcome and deal with them, might well put the wings of our souls on the fast track to heaven, having purified and perfected our souls through suffering on earth, that we may look upon the Prince of Peace, and experience eternal peace and joy with all who will reside in the glorious kingdom of heaven. Despite all that we may suffer, we can all wait in joyful hope for the coming of our Lord, when he comes to invite us to come home with him.

Appendix

A Prayer to Counter Scrupulosity

O Heavenly Father, Prince of Peace, and Loving Spirit Most Holy,

> who from mere nothingness created all the glories of the universe, things both seen and unseen,

> who gave us all the spark of earthly life,

> who gave us the hope of eternal life, through the sacrifice of the Son,

grant to us all the graces we need to overcome doubts and worries.

Help us quell temptations before they turn into sins by knowing the difference between them and the steps that can lead from one to the other.

Help us avoid all manner of deadly sins, so that we may grow in heavenly virtues.

Help us embrace your loving mercy, confident that you will pick us back up no matter how often we fall,

and in imitation of You, grant us the grace to extend like mercy to our brothers and sisters on earth who have fallen.

Let us never forget our heavenly brothers and sisters as well, calling to them for their intercession that will help still all our fears.

Give us the grace to offer up our struggles and anxieties here on earth for our suffering brethren and sisters in purgatory as they wait to gaze upon your face one day.

Open our minds to grow in faith and our hearts to grow in hope and love.

Inflame our hearts with such charity that even stone-cold scruples will dissolve and melt-away.

Open our souls to that seven-fold gift of your loving Holy Spirit, so that

> our fear of You may be grounded in filial love,

> our piety will never forget your role as Heavenly Father, and our role as important members of your Mystical Body on earth, heaven, and in purgatory,

> our knowledge of the Faith and of the things of earth will always incline us toward heaven,

our fortitude will persevere in the end as we achieve the most difficult and glorious of all goals in heaven,

our hearts will be open to the Counselor in heaven and to all the earthly counselors He guides us to for healing of our souls,

our minds will be too busy pondering the ineffable wonders of your Holy Mysteries to waste time reviewing our own petty sinful (or possibly sinful) deeds,

and all of our heart, mind, soul, and strength will be guided by your loving wisdom.

We thank you, most mysterious and holy Oneness and Threeness,

for giving us minds to reason with and souls with which to embrace the Faith,

for giving us saints and angels to guide us and pray for us as we are wayfarers on earth,

for giving us your holy Sacraments, so that we may be made members of your family; grow stronger in the faith; partake of your own Body, Blood, Soul, and Divinity; be forgiven our sins through limitless mercy; be joined with a loving second self of a spouse, if matrimony is our call; be joined with Christ if called to Holy Orders; and be healed of mental and spiritual wounds with the oils of your holy anointing.

Give us the grace and the faith to keep on praying, through written words like these, perhaps at times, and at all times through keeping our hearts and minds open to you, quieting our own fretting minds, so that we might hear your still, small voice.

Let us run to you like children when lions, tigers, bears, or scruples block our path.

Remind us to hold your mighty hand and trust in the strength of your arm, as we embrace the Holy Spirit's succulent fruits and little flowers within others.

Last of all, loving Lord,

grant us the peace and the strength we need to cast out or endure the small pebbles within our souls so that our steps will lead us and our loved ones toward you.

Amen.

Notes

Introduction

1. Jonathan S. Abramowitz, PhD, "Scrupulosity," in *Clinical Handbook of Obsessive-Compulsive Disorder and Related Problems*, ed. Jonathan S. Abramowitz, Dean McKay, and Steven Taylor (Baltimore, MD: The Johns Hopkins University Press, 2008), 157.

2. Though at times I refer to "the scrupulous," in these pages to avoid unnecessary wordiness, please bear in mind that a more accurate description would be "people with scrupulosity." We must bear in mind that a condition like scrupulosity does not define what or who a person is. I also like the ring of "scrupulous souls" which we see in our quotation from St. Alphonsus Liguori, since it reminds us that every *body* we see houses an immortal *soul,* which may well be suffering.

3. John Paul II, *Fides et Ratio*, https://www.vatican.va.

4. Thomas Aquinas, *Summa Theologica,* I-II, q.1., a.10, trans. Fathers of the English Dominican Province (Notre Dame, IN: Christian Classics [1911], 1981).

Chapter 1: Certain Sin, Possible Sin, and the Difference Between Temptation and Sin

1. Joseph W. Ciarrochi, *The Doubting Disease: Help for Scrupulosity and Religious Compulsions* (Mahwah, NJ: Paulist Press, 1995), 5.

2. "Writing in **1850**, the French psychiatrist, **Jean-Pierre Falret (1794–1870)** used the term *folie du doute*, which translates to 'madness of doubt', and in **1875** another French psychiatrist, **Henri Le Grand du Saulle (1830–1886)** published a book called *La folie du doute avec délire du toucher*, which translates to 'The madness of doubt with delirium (delusions) of touch.'" The History of OCD, OCD UK, https://www.ocduk.org/ocd/history-of-ocd/.

3. David A. Clark, *Cognitive-Behavioral Therapy for OCD and Its Subtypes,* 2nd ed. (New York: Guilford Press, 2020), 315.

4. Joseph Ciarrochi, *The Doubting Disease*, 9.

5. The History Channel, "Seven Deadly Sins," released April 28, 2009, DVD. The episode on sloth can also be found online.

6. Thomas Aquinas tells us that *vices* are tendencies, dispositions, or habits we build within ourselves to perform *sinful actions,* in just the same way that *virtues* are tendencies, dispositions, or habits we build within ourselves to perform *virtuous acts.* (An examination of the virtues that can help combat scrupulosity is in our next chapter.)

7. Kevin Vost, *You Are That Temple! A Practical Guide to Health and Holiness* (Manchester, NH: Sophia Institute Press, 2022).

8. Evagrius's list of *logismoi* in his Greek language has been translated as gluttony, fornication, avarice, distress, anger, depression, vanity, and pride.

9. John Climacus, *The Ladder of Divine Ascent* (New York: Paulist Press, 1982), 182 (as are all quotations in this section).

10. We should note as well, that *willful* denial implies that one retains one's normal intellectual capacities that serve to guide the will. A mental disorder, such as a severe clinical depressive episode or an extreme exacerbation of obsessive-compulsive scrupulosity, may lead some people to temporary thoughts of despair they would not have if

not in the throes of their psychiatric impairment. God does not deny his mercy to the ill.

11. See, for example, Bunmi O. Olatunj, Jonathan S. Abramowitz, Nathan L. Williams, Kevin M. Connolly, Jeffrey M. Lohr, "Scrupulosity and obsessive-compulsive symptoms: Confirmatory factor analysis and validity of the Penn Inventory of Scrupulosity," *Journal of Anxiety Disorders* 21 (2007): 771–787. https://my.vanderbilt.edu/earl/files/2013/11/PIS-R.pdf.

12. As cited in Ciarrochi, *The Doubting Disease*, 40. Since St. Dominic de Guzman, founder of the Order of Preachers (Dominicans), was among the earlier saints and founders of religious orders who inspired Saint Ignatius, I can't help but wonder if that "little dog" had any connections with the "dogs of the Lord," as the Dominicans were sometimes called — from *Domini* (of the Lord) and *canes* (dog) in Latin.

13. Thomas M. Santa, CSSR, *Understanding Scrupulosity: Questions and Encouragement,* 3rd ed. (Liguori, MO: Liguori Press, 2017), 26.

Chapter 2: Scrupulosity Meets the Moral Virtues

1. Cited in Trent Beatte, *Scruples and Sainthood: Accepting and Overcoming Scruples with the Help of the Saints* (Fitzwilliam, NH: Loreto Publications, 2011), 19.

2. Jesse S. Summer and Walter Sinnott-Armstrong, *Clean Hands? Philosophical Lessons from Scrupulosity* (New York: Oxford University Press, 2019), 53, citing Abramowitz, J.S. Hupper, J. D., Cohen, A. B., Tolin, D. F., & Cahill, S. P. "Religious obsessions and compulsions in a non-clinical sample: The Penn Inventory of Scrupulosity (PIOS)," *Behaviour Research and Therapy*, 40(7): 825-838.

3. Cited in Jill Haak Adels, *The Wisdom of the Saints: An Anthology* (New York: Oxford University Press, 1987), 153–154.

4. Thomas M. Santa, CSSR, *Understanding Scrupulosity*, 20.

5. Any offerings to God, especially the offering of the Eucharistic Sacrifice during Mass.

6. The ancient practice of offering the fruits of the season's first agricultural harvests to God. (And no, we are not required or expected to grow gardens and literally do this today!)

7. And in an amazing coincidence (or perhaps, "Godincidence"), readers of my previous book, *Unearthing Your Ten Talents,* might recall that I first happened to write about King as a champion of justice on Monday, January 21, 2008, which was in that year also his national holiday!

8. There are a host of recent scientific articles on gratitude as an aspect of psychotherapy. Indeed, an Existential Gratitude Scale (EGS) has recently been developed. See for example, Lilian Jans-Beken & Paul T.P. Wong, "Development and preliminary validation of the Existential Gratitude Scale (EGS)," *Counseling Psychology Quarterly,* 37, no. I (2021): https://doi.org/10.1080/09515070.2019.1656054.

9. Joseph Ciarrochi, *The Doubting Disease,* 15.

10. See Kevin Vost, *Memorize the Faith, Memorize the Reasons, Memorize the Mass, Memorize the Latin Mass, Memorize the Stoics.*

11. Jill Haak Adels, *The Wisdom of the Saints,* 154.

12. It's a line from Alexander Pope's *An Essay on Criticism* from the early 1700s.

13. It's been traced to a book from around 1350.

14. My thanks to Rhonda Ortiz for this insight.

15. David A. Clark, *Cognitive-Behavioral Therapy for OCD and Its Subtypes* (New York: The Guilford Press, 2020), viii.

16. Obsessive-Compulsive Disorder, National Institute of Mental Health, https://www.nimh.nih.gov/health/statistics/obsessive-compulsive-disorder-ocd.

17. Teacher, from the Latin *docere,* "to teach." Indeed, he has been declared the *Doctor Zelantissimus* ("Most Zealous Doctor"). The Church has also deemed him the "Prince of Moral Theologians," and a patron of confessors.

18. Thomas Santa, *Understanding Scrupulosity,* 29.

19. Alphonsus Liguori, *The True Spouse of Jesus Christ: The Com-*

plete Works of Saint Alphonsus Liguori (The Redemptorist Father's Press, 1929), 545.

20. Alphonsus Liguori, *The Glories of Mary* (New York: P.J. Kennedy & Sons, 1888), https://www.ecatholic2000.com/liguori/glories45.shtml.

Chapter 3: Love Conquers All — Including Scrupulosity

1. Thomas Aquinas, *Treatise on the Two Commandments of Charity and the Ten Commandments of the Laws,* trans. Father Rawes, D.D. (London: Burns and Oats, 1880), 2.

2. Thomas Aquinas, *Treatise on the Two Commandments*, 2.

3. Ibid., 4.

4. Fact sheet on Scrupulosity: https://iocdf.org/wp-content/uploads/2014/10/IOCDF-Scrupulosity-Fact-Sheet.pdf.

5. Gerald Nestadt, Marco Grados, and J F Samuels, "Genetics of OCD," *Psychiatric Clinics of North America,* 33, no. 1 (March 2010): 141–158, doi: 10.1016/j.psc.2009.11.001. https://www.ncbi.nlm.nih.gov/pmc/articles/PMC2824902/. (All of the remaining biological findings cited in this essay were derived from this article unless otherwise noted.)

6. Op. cit..

7. Ibid.

8. As cited, for example, in David Clark's *Cognitive-Behavioral Therapy for OCD and Its Subtypes*, 316.

9. Kyle N. Weir, Ph.D., LMFT, *Saints Overcoming Scrupulosity: Embracing Truths About Mental Illness And The Restored Gospel In Treating Religious-Oriented Obsessive-Compulsive Disorder* (Washington, UT: Finegold Creek Press, 2021).

10. Summers and Sinnott-Armstrong, *Clean Hands,* 44–47.

11. Obsessive-Compulsive Disorder (OCD), Mayo Clinic. https://www.mayoclinic.org/diseases-conditions/obsessive-compulsive-disorder/symptoms-causes/syc-20354432.

12. Quoted with permission from Michael Baker.

Chapter 4: The Holy Spirit Gives Gifts to the Scrupulous

1. Gregory the Great, *The Homilies on the Prophet Ezekiel*, II 7, 7. St. Robert Bellarmine (1642–1721) also explicitly compared the seven gifts to a ladder, the bottom step resting on the earth with fear of the Lord, and the top step touching heaven through the spirit of wisdom.

2. So you need not look back: "You who fear the Lord, trust in him, and your reward will not fail; you who fear the Lord, hope for good things, for everlasting joy and mercy. You who fear the Lord, love him, and your hearts will be made radiant" (Sir 2:8–10).

3. CSSp stands for Congregation of the Holy Ghost under the protection of the Immaculate Heart of Mary.

4. Bernard J. Kelly, CSSp, *The Seven Gifts* (New York: Sheed and Ward, 1942), 96.

5. Bernard Kelly, *The Seven Gifts*, 97–98.

6. Bonaventure, *Collations on the Seven Gifts of the Holy Spirit*, trans. Zachary Hayes, O.F.M. (Saint Bonaventure, NY: Franciscan Institute Publications, 2008), 36 (referencing 1 Cor 15:10).

7. Bernard Kelly, *The Seven Gifts*.

8. Louis of Granada, *The Sinner's Guide* (Veritatis Splendor Publications, 2012), 289.

9. Reginald Garrigou-Lagrange, O.P., *The Theological Virtues, Volume One, ON FAITH*, trans. Thomas a Kempis Reilly, O.P. (St. Louis: Herder Book Co., 1965), 393.

10. Bonaventure, *Collations on the Seven Gifts of the Holy Spirit*.

11. From St. Alphonsus Liguouri's prayer for the gifts of the Holy Spirit.

12. "For the reasoning of mortals is worthless, and our designs are likely to fail" (RSV2CE).

13. John of Saint Thomas, *The Gifts of the Holy Ghost*, 161.

14. Ernest F. Latko, OFM, S.T.D., "A Psychotherapy for Scruples,"

Catholic Culture, https://www.catholicculture.org/culture/library/view .cfm?recnum=7907.

15. Bonaventure, *Collations*, 152. Per the RSV-2CE, "Let those that are at peace with you be many, but let your advisers be one in a thousand" (Sir 6:6).

16. Reginald Garrigou-Lagrange, *The Theological Virtues,* 396.

17. Ibid.

18. David Clark, *Cognitive-Behavioral Therapy*, 84–85.

19. Ibid., 78.

20. See, for examples, Ciarrochi's *The Doubting Disease*, Clark's *Cognitive-Behavioral Therapy for OCD and Its Subtypes* (2nd ed), Davidson's *Daring to Challenge OCD,* and Summers and Sinnott-Armstrong's *Clean Hands.*

21. David Clark, *Cognitive-Behavioral Therapy*, 101.

22. I'll note as well that today one can use the internet to find networks of Catholic therapists and counselors across the nation. Further, one's priest may know a good one in one's own area.

23. Sisters of the Blessed Sacrament, https://www.newadvent.org /cathen/02599a.htm. It has been reported that St. Katherine Drexel donated approximately $20 million dollars to her order and various charities over her lifetime. See Tim Smith, "How a Saint Became Part of the Tax Code, Forever Changing Philanthropy, *Catholic News Service*, March 28, 2022, https://www.thecompassnews.org/2022/03/how-a-saint -became-part-of-the-tax-code-forever-changing-u-s-philanthropy.

Chapter 5: Scrupulosity and the Healing Power of the Sacraments

1. Thomas Santa, *Understanding Scrupulosity*, 108.

2. This appears to have been the case for the man who led a movement against the Church and abolished all but the Sacraments of Baptism, Eucharist, and Penance within his own church. I refer to the former Augustinian monk, Martin Luther (1483–1586). For a theological analysis see "Martin Luther," https://www.catholic.com/encyclopedia

/martin-luther. For a detailed psychoanalysis (or psychohistory) see the book by renowned psychoanalyst Erik Erikson, *Young Man Luther* (W. H. Norton & Co.).

3. I'll note as well that some of the general background material on the sacraments in this chapter draws from material I first prepared for an introduction to and summary of the *Summa Theologica* I wrote called *The One-Minute Aquinas* (Sophia Institute Press, 2014).

4. Thomas also cites Romans 6:3: "Do you not know that all of us who have been baptized into Christ Jesus were baptized into his death?"

5. Though I will note that in a helpful modern psychological book on the treatment of OCD, a case is presented of a former priest who had scrupulous thoughts that he had somehow inadvertently performed invalid baptisms. See Joan Davidson, Ph.D., *Daring to Challenge OCD: Overcome Your Fear of Treatment & Take Control of Your Life Using Exposure and Response Prevention* (Oakland, CA: New Harbinger Publications, 2014).

6. The "etc." means they also explicitly name the Son and the Holy Spirit too. That this remains the case in the Latin and Eastern liturgies today can be seen in the CCC 1240. Christ's original instructions went like this: "Go therefore and make disciples of all nations, baptizing them in the name of the Father and of the Son and of the Holy Spirit" (Mt 28:19).

7. Since I first wrote these lines in January 2022, a prominent case has come out in which it was determined that a priest in the U.S. did administer invalid baptisms by declaring "We baptize ..." instead of "I baptize." The "I" used in the proper ritual means that the person baptizing does so in the name of Jesus Christ. While people who were known to have been baptized invalidly were advised to be rebaptized, I cannot help agreeing with a modern orthodox Catholic apologist who opined that God would never send a person to hell "on a technicality." Further, the incidence of such invalid baptisms is likely very small. None of us should worry about or investigate our own baptism

ceremony. See also the following information in this text on baptism, including "baptism of desire."

8. Also see CCC 1258, 1260, 1281 on "Baptism of desire."

9. Cited in Thomas Santa, *Understanding Scrupulosity*, 114.

10. Ibid., 115 for direct quotation. Attributed to St. Philip Neri in Jill Haak Adels, *Wisdom of the Saints*, 155.

11. Thomas Santa, *Understanding Scrupulosity*, 110.

12. Compare to the words of the Invitation to Communion at Mass and the centurion's words in Matthew 8:8 & Luke 7:7.

13. Honorary titles given to Saint Thomas over the centuries from Pope John XXII in the fourteenth century to Pope St. John Paul II in the twentieth are the "Common Doctor" (common to all the Church), "Angelic Doctor" (for his treatise on the angels), "Eucharistic Doctor" (for his writings on transubstantiation and the Eucharist), and the "Humanistic Doctor" (for his writings on the nature, dignity, virtues, and happiness of humanity).

14. From *Sacris Solemnis, Juncta Sint Gaudia* (Let Joys Be Joined to Solemn Feasts), in Robert Anderson and Johann Moser, trans. & eds., *The Aquinas Prayer Book: The Hymns and Prayers of Saint Thomas Aquinas* (Manchester, NH: Sophia Institute Press, 2000), 95.

15. Robert Anderson and Johann Moser, *The Aquinas Prayer Book*, 69.

16. Used with permission from Fr. Wade Menezes, CPM. "Ten Commandments For Those Who Struggle With Scrupulosity" https:// fathersofmercy.com/ten-commandments-for-those-who-struggle -with-scrupulosity/. Readers are also directed to his third chapter "The Sacrament of Penance and Reconciliation" in Fr. Wade Menezes, CPM, *Overcoming the Evil Within: The Reality of Sin and the Trans- forming Power of God's Grace and Mercy* (Irondale, AL: EWTN Press, 2020). Father Wade also calls the sacrament a "Sacrament of Mercy" or "Tribunal of Mercy" because our Lord referred to confession as the "Tribunal of Mercy" twice to Saint Faustina, which she records in her *Diary* in paragraphs 975 and 1488.

17. See chapter 13, "Ten Commandments for the Scrupulous," in Thomas Santa, *Understanding Scrupulosity.* The latest online version is here: https://scrupulousanonymous.org/wp-content/uploads/2015/10 /Ten_Commandments_for_the_Scrupulous_2013.pdf.

18. Thomas Santa, *Understanding Scrupulosity*, 9.

19. CCC 1423 as cited above, and Mt 5:24.

20. Summers and Sinnott-Armstrong, *Clean Hands,* 186.

21. Citing Aristotle's *Nichomachean Ethics,* book 8, ch. 12.

22. From Rufus's Lecture 13, for example, in Cora Lutz, *Musonius Rufus Fragments* (New Deli, India: Isha Books, 2013). Readers are invited to compare his insights, based on human reason and natural law, to CCC 2366–2367, 2360–2362.

23. David Clark, *Cognitive-Behavioral Therapy*, 27, citing previous research of the Obsessive-Compulsive Cognitions Working Group.

24. You can easily find the original tune sung by Luciano Pavarotti and others online.

25. "St. Veronica Giuliani–Mystic, Stigmatic, Victim Soul, Incorruptable." https://www.mysticsofthechurch.com/2015/07/st-veronica -giuliani-extraordinary.html.

26. "The awesome power of the Most Holy Eucharist in the life and words of Saint Veronica Giuliani." https://rorate-caeli.blogspot .com/2011/08/saint-veronica-giuliani-and-most-holy.html.

27. Ibid.

Chapter 6: The Power of Pure Prayer (Even If We're Not Paying Attention Very Well!)

1. Though indeed, Jesus Christ, as God willingly made man, did in his humanity pray to God the Father that he would follow the Father's will, even unto his death on the cross.

2. For a whole host of insights on our guardian angels, see Thomas's wonderful question of eight articles, "Of the Guardianship of the Good Angels," *ST*, I, q.113.

3. Rom 15:30–32; 2 Cor 1:10–11; Eph 6:18–20; Phil 1:19; Col

4:2–4; 1 Thes 5:24; 2 Thes 3:1–2.

4. As cited in Thomas Santa, *Understanding Scrupulosity*, 123.

5. Joseph A. Knowles, *Saint Brigid: Patroness of Ireland* (Dublin: Brown and Nolan, 1907; reprinted by Kessinger Publishing, LCC, 2009), 94. Versions of this story also appear in ancient lives of Saint Patrick. I first recounted Brigid's vision in my book *Three Irish Saints* (Charlotte, NC: TAN Books, 2012), 146–147.

6. Kyle Weir, *Saints Overcoming Scrupulosity*, 10.

7. Steven C. Hayes, Kirk D. Strosahl, and Kelly G. Wilson, *Acceptance and Commitment Therapy: The Process and Practice of Mindful Change* (New York: The Guilford Press, 2012).

8. This article provides a brief overview. "Dialectical Behavior Therapy," *Psychology Today,* https://www.psychologytoday.com/us /therapy-types/dialectical-behavior-therapy.

9. Jeffery M. Schwartz, MD, with Beverly Beyette, *Brain Lock: Free Yourself from Obsessive-Compulsive Behavior,* 20th anniversary edition (New York: Harper Perennial, 2016), 207. I can't help but think how far ahead of their time were some of those ancient Stoics who would give rise to cognitive therapies nearly two millennia after they were gone. Epictetus, for example, said (in my own translation of his *Handbook*, ch. 1): "From the start, make it your habit to say to each harsh impression, 'You are an impression and not at all what you at first appear to be.' Next, examine and test it by the rules you have learned, first and foremost by whether it has to do with things that are under our control or not. If it regards something outside of your control, be ready to say, 'You are nothing to me!'"

10. Jeffery Schwartz and Beverly Beyette, *Brain Lock*, 208.

Chapter 7: Christ Loves All Who Are Burdened and Yearns to Lighten Their Yokes

1. Aelred of Rievaulx, *The Mirror of Charity,* trans. Elizabeth Connor (Kalamazoo, MI: Cistercian Publications, 1990), 133.

2. In addressing scrupulosity among members of The Church of

Jesus Christ of Latter-Day Saints (Mormons), counselor Kyle N. Weir, Ph.D. addresses this common issue in his *Saints Overcoming Scrupulosity*, 8–9.

3. For a listing and analysis of all seven "last words" and how they all served to combat the seven deadly sins, see Fulton J. Sheen, *The Seven Capital Sins* (New York: Alba House, 2001). For those interested in a quick listing, numbers 1 and 2 are in the text and the rest are as follows: 3) "Woman, behold, your son! … Behold, your mother! (Jn 19:26–27); 4) "My God, my God, why have you forsaken me?" (Mt 27:46; Mk 15:34); 5) "I thirst." (Jn 19:28); 6) "It is finished." (Jn 19:30); and 7) "Father, into your hands I commit my spirit!" (Lk 23:46).

4. Not surprisingly, since his name itself meant "Golden -mouthed" in Greek!

5. As cited in St. Thomas Aquinas, *Catena Aurea,* vol. I, part II, *The Gospel of Saint Matthew,* trans. John Henry Newman (New York: Cosimo Classics, 2007), 428.

6. In Robert Anderson and Johann Moser, *The Aquinas Prayer Book,* 97.

7. As cited in Mary Carruthers, *The Book of Memory: A Study of Memory in Medieval Culture* (Cambridge, MA: Cambridge University Press, 1990), 44.

8. https://integratedcatholiclife.org/2019/10/scruples-and-moderation -understanding-the-advice-of-st-ignatius-of-loyola/.

9. https://rhondaortiz.com/scripture-for-the-scrupulous.

10. Francis de Sales, *Introduction to the Devout Life: A Popular Abridgment* by Madame Yvonne Stephan (Rockford, IL: TAN Books, 1990), part 3, chapter 9, 152.

11. Francis de Sales, *Introduction to the Devout Life*, part 3, chapter 10, 156–157.

12. Ibid., part 4, chapter 7, as cited in Fr. Raymond's *Spiritual Director and Physician,* 171 (referencing Mt 26:41).

About the Author

Kevin Vost (1961–2023) obtained his doctorate in clinical psychology (Psy.D.) from Adler University in Chicago, with internship and dissertation at the SIU School of Medicine Alzheimer Center's Memory and Aging Clinic. He taught psychology at schools including the University of Illinois at Springfield and Aquinas College in Nashville, Tennessee, and spent 32 years in the adjudication of mental and physical disability claims for the Social Security Administration. Kevin authored over two dozen books. Kevin and his wife Kathy were married for 39 years, and had two sons and five grandchildren.